The

Introduction to the

Mindset

Of the

Apostle Luke

Written by,
Rev. Dr. Derrick A. Hill
www.oncommonground.freewebspace.com
revdrderrickhill@yahoo.com

We are about to embark on a journey that I can only describe as a walk through the present of God himself. This particular book will take us through the mindset of the Apostle Luke by way of the development of his true essence by understanding the written word. This will place us in the position to see as he saw and feel as he feels to better understand the particular written word of God that the Apostle Luke was lead by the Spirit of God to write. This is most interesting because if we can understand the make up of the Apostle Luke then I can walk through the developing usage of the primary traits that brought him to the position of being a tool use by God to produce an effective product that has advanced the kingdom of God. In that we find our heart desire to be used by God in some shape form or fashion to help edify the kingdom of God and to glorify God all in the same motion. As we take our journey we will fine ourselves as well in the midst of the journey.

This is the source that drives me to write this particular book for us as the Body of Christ to fine ourselves within the scriptures and make up of our traits to better understand our character to see the position that God is placing us in. Within that we have the opportunity to understand better ourselves and the developing process to mold us into the person God wants us to be. In doing this we will also be able to see where we have gotten off path as well as see how come our road have been so difficult to us as well some will even find out why we have been stuck in the same place for so long. In growth there are stages that must be develop as well as placement that have to met within the fine woven thread of God's master plan for our lives. Now what will be even so interesting that God knows our heart and mind and action before we even make a move in this we have to realize that our mental mindset is the avenue which brings this about by way of understanding one's character tells us a lot about the person. What if you can map out your character and know where to work on and how to work on it to build a connection in the weak to the strengthener above. How helpful would this be to you as you grow spiritually as well as physically?

Within the Apostle Luke journey the importance of his development was the closeness he got to Christ Jesus. This is the same formula you and I have to comprehend to understand the severity of becoming a vessel that is willing and able to be used by God in a mighty way. The positioning of this particular gospel will reveal a great deal about the overall complexity of the building process. We need to develop a mentality that embraces the process instead of one that is running through the process and never full understanding the mechanics of the process and learning from the different situations, circumstances, and events. We are so caught up as a people on the outcome that we over look the entire process to see the moving of the hand of God, even when we feel that He is not moving at all. In this we embrace the trials and tribulations that helps mold us on one level to help us deal with what is coming on the next level. In the mindset of the Apostle Luke there will be some uncovering of the adversary that we might have missed in our lives that been holding us back from accomplishing the necessary things need to become a mega force in the Body of Christ.

You and I have to stay teachable in order to stay in the position of taking on more and more within the Body of Christ. Some might say that I am comfortable where I am in the Body of Christ and I don't want to take on any more and that is very interesting. Simply because we are not programmer of our faith but we are the receivers of the well laid plan of God that wants us to the fullest of potential forewhich He created us to be. If we chose to stop where we fill comfortable what happens to the lives that in the next position that only you can touch, that only you as the vessel which God has chosen to reach them. Better yet the product that you can produce within moving to the next level that can edify the Body of Christ and glorify God what happens to that if we choose only to stay comfortable in our position that we are in. There is so much depending on you that comfortable have to be within the Lord where we fine our rest not in the position that we are in. You see if God calls you for His purpose then it is His plan that we are following and not our will that controls God's plan.

Let see how this works as we come to God by His calling by His mercy and grace then God has a purpose for our life. In that purpose there is development stages that we have to reach to be prepared for the position forewhich God has called us to. In this movement of getting there we have to learn more and more to submit to the will of God and take our will and sacrifice it unto the Lord. Simply because our will is tainted with the penetration of the adversary and we fully don't know the entire plan of God, in that we fine ourselves to be molded and folded and moved along as we are developing that is revealing our spiritual gifts and we begin to see our hearts desire. In seeing our hearts desire forewhich God has placed there we have to develop the right type of attitude as well as manner and character to be fully functioning in that position. Here is the interesting part most of the time our position is in a place forewhich by physical system of things we are not qualified to do by paper knowledge. But the desire that is in our hearts overwhelms and developed by God and shaped and molded by him supercedes the paper and the favor of God places you in that position and you become productive in that area as if you have been train and schooled in that area.

But what is so unfortunate that most members of the Body of Christ do not reach their full potential simply because they fight the process and turn away from the will of God to stay in the position they are in out of fear and reservation as well as deep penetration of the adversary illusion. In this we will look deep within the character make up of the Apostle Luke and see the different developments that takes place that gives strength to one to fulfill his or hers true destiny within the Body of Christ. In this we will see how come one does not meet their destiny as well as see how one reaches their destiny. In this we will find ourselves and see where we are within the will of God to do two things. One get back on track if I am off and secondly start moving in the will of God and submit myself in my weak areas to the will of God to start moving.

Within this material we will look at those that are linked to the Apostle Luke that will reveal the essence of the purity of God's word that is releasing revelation unto us. In that we pull down the atmosphere of God by attaching the principles to the revelation forewhich you and I implement in our lives to develop by molding of God to the vessel needed to be used for His plan. We are going together to search the word of God to look for the proper positioning of this particular gospel as well as the mindset that it took for the Apostle Luke to become who he was in the true form. In other words what did the Apostle Luke have and know that develop him in such a way the produce an effective product that edified the Body of Christ and glorified God. This will be important to us to see the different levels as well as to find ourselves in the word of God. The Apostle Luke possessed a particular character that is so important and crucial to us in our growing in the power of God as well as spiritually to affect the physical that will cause a product to be produced that will edify the Body of Christ and glorify God.

The Apostle Luke took hold to a principle that shook the very foundation of hell itself and applied it in his life to be used by God to bring the same principle unto you and I so we can receive our blessing in this area. This particular book "The Introduction to the Mindset of the Apostle Luke" will cover an area so important to the Body of Christ that it is impossible to put into words. We have to see the Apostle Luke mindset in order to receive the fullness of this particular area to produce an effective product in us that truly edifies the Body of Christ and glorify God to the point where others will most definitely cry out what must I do in order to be saved. So sit back and let us come together in search of the fundamental principle that holds the very key to our productivity than any thing else.

Background

Now let us begin with the understanding of the direction we are going in and get the fullness of the area, which will be covered. The Bible is separated into two parts that ultimately is placing more attention to one part than the other. I prefer to look at the Bible as one continuing book of life that brings forth a continuing work of God to show us through both past and present our destiny and the ability to function today and our destiny of tomorrow. In this I truly get the entire revelation forewhich gives a beautiful revelation of the word of God. In this the Old Testament is brought forth in the New Testament that gives utterance to the true essence of the word of God where each word inspires and give true meaning for us today. If we don't see the word of God in this form we miss the essence of purity of the word of God we fully don't get everything that God intended for us to receive from the word. I am not so full of myself that I believe I hold the model lock on how to study the word of God but I am convince that we must bring together the Old and New Testament to receive the fullness of the word of God.

Now this you will see here in this particular book about the Apostle Luke simply because I will travel from the Old to the New in order to reach the present and ultimately the future. This will be a very interesting challenge for you and I to come together and receive the blessing that God has for us as we go through the scriptures and see the fullness of God's intention for you and I. So let us get started. To better understand the Apostle Luke is to see how the connection was formulated in the writing of the Apostle Luke to formulate a productive product that has inspired millions in the Body of Christ. Let us take a look within the word of God to see the building of a character that is so essential to all of us that God made it a mandate that all must have that shows evidence of Him in our lives.

Now God opens a vision to us within His ultimate plan for us to see the growing of the character forewhich you and I have to see in order to see where we are in the process. So let us look at how God's plan unfolds for you and I to receive the revelation of the writings of the Apostle Luke. First and foremost we have to understand the positioning forewhich God place this particular character in the plan of God and the order forewhich gives great revelation. Look at how the Bible places the revelation for you and I: The Bible says: On the south side shall be the standard of the camp of Reuben according to their armies: and the captain of the children of Reuben shall be E-li'-zur the son of Shed'-e-ur. And his host, and those that were numbered thereof, were forty and six thousand and five hundred. And those which pitch by him shall be the tribe of Simeon: and the captain of the children of Simeon shall be She-lu'-mi-el the son of Zu-ri-shad'-dai. And his host, and those that were numbered of them, were fifty and nine thousand and three hundred. Then the tribe of Gad: and the captain of the sons of God shall be E-li'-a-saph the son of Reu'-el. And his host, and those that were numbered of them, were forty and five thousand and six hundred and fifty. All that were numbered in the camp of Reuben were an hundred thousand and fifty and one thousand and four hundred and fifty, throughout their armies. And they shall set forth in the second rank. (Numbers 2:10-16)

In the essence of those scriptures is when the children of Israel was in the wilderness God spoke Moses and Aaron saying: The Bible says: And the Lord spake unto Moses and unto Aaron, saying, Every man of the children of Israel shall pitch by his own standard, with the ensign of their father's house: far off about the tabernacle of the congregation shall they pitch. (Numbers: 2:1-2) So separation was by the Lord according to His divine plan that is being released within the Tribes of Israel for us today. This is very important for you and I to understand because there is something within the separation because it was the division of the entire being into parts that held the essence of traits that developed a character that holds the secret to the miraculous character of Jesus Christ. Here in the separation God is revealing unto us not only the number of the members in the household but also the traits of the father of the tribe. This is the key to the revelation that is hidden deep within the fathers of the tribe that spread forth and came to their fullness in Christ Jesus.

You see this is the direct link to us and to Jesus Christ our character that comes forth after hearing and acting on the word of God in our lives. In this God was giving us a blueprint of the traits that produces the character of Christ in our lives in order to move up to the next level that God have for us. Also within the separation we will see the developing of the traits that gives the functioning tools necessary for the character to come forth within the stages of growth. In other words we have to understand ourselves and how we build our own character through the developing of our father's fathers that moves us toward the positioning of our own character. We are going to see the positioning influences over the character building traits that link the fullness of the scriptures and transform them in to life. You see the scripture will help us see the connection between the two the Old and New as they reveal us in away that we can understand, how to get out of this, why this is happening to me, and what I need to work on? If we can see the positioning of these tribes and understand that God separated them for a particular reason that is to edify the Body of Christ by the building of the character of Jesus Christ.

You see if you have not had a chance to read the rest of the books in the series of the Introduction to the Mindset of the Apostle Matthew and the Apostle Mark then I need to catch you up here. First the Apostle Matthew called to remembrance to the Jewish Community the Kingship of Christ in that is the king mentality. The Apostle Mark was lead by the spirit to write about the Servant or Servitude of Christ. Once the mindset is focus on the Heavenly Host to renew our thinking brings forth the kingship mentality in that we start building a connection from the mind to the heart. Were the heart is being tenderize by the renewing of the mind which gives us a picture of Christ heart. A heart of service that triggers us to this point of where we are and this is what is produced when we are hitting on all cylinders and seeking first the kingdom of God.

Now we have to understand that our traits are develop through the actions we take in different situations and circumstance that have been influence by others in our life as well as our own interpretation of life. In this we are subject to growth and change as we go through life but the key here is the influence of the word of God and the impact forewhich we implement the word of God in our lives. To remove the false illusions of the adversary and see clearly how the deep penetration of the adversary attacks that triggers our emotions and thoughts and how we react to them. In this we see that the Apostle Luke has develop in a way that moved through the building of the Body of Christ with great impact. As well he is surround by a particular group that will uncover the mindset of the Apostle Luke by way of the situations and circumstance of the past that influence him and those that are around him. We have to remember that we as human flesh we pass down things to our offspring forewhich some don't even know how to deal with it when we see ourselves in our child.

They begin to act like us and talk like us and walk like us and in a lot of cases begin to think like us because we are the receivers of DNA that matches our ancestors and we have to deal with some things that have been passed down. In that we have to be able to link with something that can help me take what was passed down and then mold that with my own processing center against what I am seeing and give birth to a productive product that edifies and glorifies all within the same motion. For some this sounds very strange and to others it sounds like an impossible task but we have to remember we have an awesome God that have the model lock on how to mold us to become a willing vessel to be used for God. But we have to open, willing, obedient as well as sold out for Jesus that we refuse to do anything without Jesus Christ in it. In that we are developing and sometimes even destroying things in our lives that is pulling us away from our destiny. In remembering that we are developing we also have to put away something as we grow spiritually and move into a deeper relationship with the Lord.

As we mature we put away childish things because now we are simply growing spiritually and in that will bring on new challenges as well as more attacks from the adversary and as well more responsibility. Now some refuse to take this movement in their lives but in that case we see the journey in the wilderness taking over. Going around and around the mountain and not progressing and constantly repeating the same situations and circumstances until they realize that God has a place for them in the Body of Christ and maturity is the key to finding it. You and I is called to stay in the word and it is evidence that we are His disciples and we will know the truth and the truth will set us free and this is our calling to maturity.

The Apostle Luke coming to the fullness of God's development brought forth a character that is so important to you and I that we need to understand it and see it in motion so we first can see how much work we have to do to get there. And secondly we have to be able to remove the adversary stumbling blocks that are before us and shake off the deep penetration of the adversary on how I think and react in certain situations and circumstances. The Apostle Luke is credited to two books in the Bible, The Gospel of Luke and Acts. In this many questions might come to you or for some might not. But for me I wanted to know how come The Apostle Luke was used? How come he wrote in a particular manner? How come it was simply place where it was and what did it have to do with me? Now here is one where many people say, "How come all the gospel basically talks about the same thing?" Now you might have develop a few questions now yourself and I want you to know that we are going to look some of these questions as well as others and I pray that we address your questions as well. Let us get started by saying that each gospel has a particular place within the Body of Christ base upon the perception we look upon the gospels.

If we take the gospels in the context, which it was written, then we receive revelation that we would not receive if we just look at them as writings. In other words if we understand the mindset of the writers and see the connection between the Old and New Testament and understand the positioning then we open the door to and new look instead of the look of just seeing words. Remember that each word of God is inspired to move something either within you, around you and for you. In this we look for the true essence of the word of God and now we are looking for the direct link between the Old and New Testament. In this we are going to address some of the questions that have been released. So let us get started.

Reuben

Now we are starting here for a particular reason. On the southside of the tabernacle God divided here three tribes and I want to look at them to see their development and see if it got anything to do with me. Most of all I want to see what it has to do with the Apostle Luke and the movement in the spiritual realm that caused God to reach down and place this within the word of God. Now Reuben means: "behold a son" and was the first born of Jacob born to Leah in Padan Aram. Now the birth of Reuben and the situation and place of his birth was very interesting in the developing of Reuben or growing of Reuben. Padan Aram is in the Upper Mesopotamia around Haran and the home of the patriarch Abraham after he moved from Ur of the Chaldeans. And even later Abraham sent his servant to Padan Aram to find a bride for his son Issac. Now in this bride that his servants brought back Jacob was born. As well what is so interesting about this is that this is the same place where Jacob avoid the wrath of his brother Esau who was born at Padan Aram Jacob twin brother.

Now that situation was going on within the land and between the brothers but there was another situation going on as well and this was the love that was being sought by Leah from her husband. But there was a significant situation that based the love issue into blossom that cause a rippling effect within the household of Jacob. Let us take a look at what the Bible says: Then Jacob went on his journey, and came into the land of the people of the east. And he looked, and behold a well in the field, and, lo, there were three flocks of sheep lying by it; for out of that well they watered the flocks: and a great stone was upon the well's mouth. And thither were all the flocks gathered: and they rolled the stone from the well's mouth, and watered the sheep, and put the stone again upon the well's mouth in his place. And Jacob said unto them, My brethren, whence be ye? And they said, Of Ha'-ran are we. And he said unto them, know ye Laban the son of Na'-hor? And they said, We know him.

And he said unto them, Is he well? And they said, He is well: and, behold, Ra'-chel his daughter cometh with the sheep. And he said, Lo, it is yet high day, neither is it time that the cattle should be gathered together: water ye the sheep, and go and feed them. And they said, We cannot, until all the flocks be gathered together, and till they roll the stone from the well's mouth; then we water the sheep. And while he yet spake with them, Ra'-chel came with her father's sheep: for she kept them. And it came to pass, when Jacob saw Ra'chel the daughter of Laban his mother's brother, and the sheep of Laban his mother's brother, that Jacob went near, and rolled the stone from the well's mouth, and watered the flock of Laban his mother's brother. And Jacob kissed Ra'-chel, and lifted up his voice and wept. And Jacob told Ra'-chel that he was her father's brother, and that he was Rebekah's son: and she ran and told her father. And it came to pass, when Laban heard the tidings of Jacob his sister's son, that he ran to meet him, and embraced him, and kissed him, and brought him to his house. And he told Laban all these things. And Laban said to him. Surely thou art my bone and my flesh. And he abode with him the space of a month.

And Laban said unto Jacob, Because thou art my brother, shouldest thou therefore serve me for nought? tell me, what shall thy wages be? And

Laban had two daughters: the name of the elder was Leah, and the name of the younger was Ra'-chel. Leah was tender eyed: but Ra'-chel was beautiful and well favoured. And Jacob loved Ra'-chel: and said I will thee seven years for Ra'-chel thy younger daughter. And Laban said, It is better that I give her to thee, than that I should give her to another man: abide with me. And Jacob served seven years for Ra'-chel; and they seemed unto him but a few days, for the love he had to her. And Jacob said unto Laban, Give me my wife, for my days are fulfilled, that I may go in unto her. And Laban gathered together all the men of the place, and made a feast.

And it came to pass in the evening that he took Leah his daughter, and brought her to him; and he went in unto her. And Laban gave unto his daughter Leah Zil'-pah his maid for an handmaid. And it came to pass, that in the morning, behold, it was Leah: and he said to Laban, What is this thou hast done unto me? did not I serve with thee for Ra'-chel? Wherefore then hast thou beguiled me? And Laban said, It must not be so done in our country, to give the younger before the firstborn. Fulfil her week, and we will give thee this also for the service which thou shalt serve with me yet seven other years. And Jacob did so, and fulfilled her week: and he gave him Ra'-chel his daughter Bil'-hah his handmaid to be her maid. And he went n also unto Ra'-chel, and he loved also Ra'-chel more than Leah, and served with him yet seven other years. And when the Lord saw that Leah was hated he opened her womb: but Ra'-chel was barren. And Leah conceived, and bare a son, and she called his name Reuben: for she said, Surely the Lord hath looked upon my affliction; now therefore my husband will love me. (Genesis 29: 1-32)

Now in the under current of the entire section of scriptures or verses we see that because of Jacob love for one over another cost him a position to be deceived by Laban. As well as God intervene and showed favor unto Leah to bore the first born son Reuben and Leah deem that God showed this favor because God saw that she was hated because of the deception which placed her in the situation. In that she was given the heritance of Jacob through the firstborn son, which was born in the midst of the uproar that was going on between the women for the love of Jacob. Now this is very interesting simply because what was suppose to be was not. Reuben being the first-born saw first hand the fighting between the women and felt the tension between the households of Jacob that influence him greatly. The Bible speaks very little of the up bringing of Reuben but it do gives a great account of a situation that took place that was a continuing battle between Leah and Rachel. In this particular situation God intervene and growth within the women was building in way of the spirit instead of the physical simply because they was caring this burden of love within them.

Let us take a look at what the Bible says: And Reuben went in the days of wheat harvest, and found mandrakes in the field, and brought them unto his mother Leah. Then Ra'-chel said to Leah, Give me, I pray thee, thy son's mandrakes. And she said unto her, Is it a small matter that thou hast taken my husband? and wouldest thou take away my son's mandrakes also? And Ra'-chel said, Therefore he shall lie with thee to night for thy son's mandrakes. And Jacob came out of the field in the evening, and Leah went out to meet him, and said, Thou must come in unto me; for surely I have hired thee with my son's mandrakes. And he lay with her that night. And God hearkened unto Leah, and she conceived, and bare Jacob the fifth son. And Leah said, God hath given me my hire, because I have given my maiden to my husband: and she called his name Is'-sa-char. (Genesis 30: 14-17)

Now before we get into this I want you to see the meaning of the name Issachar, which is "there is hire or reward" that indicate a great revelation within the understanding of the entire situation. Let me explain this was the ninth son of Jacob but also the fifth son by Leah, but what was so interesting by this whole thing that Rachel was barren all this time. She has given birth to no children and the mandrake plant is fruit producing plant with dark green leaves and small bluish-purple flowers that brought forth a yellow fruit that is small sweet-tasting, and fragrant. It had narcotic qualities and could have been used as a medicine but also it was considered a love potion. Now when Reuben brought the mandrake fruit home to his mother and Rachel saw it this was her way of breaking the barren situation she was in. But also Leah already had produced four sons and places this fruit as if a wagering bargin to have Jacob come unto her. Yes she places her trust in the Lord but use the situation to hire her own husband for a night.

Now in this God rewarded the faithfulness of Leah by leaning on the Lord for her childbearing and produced a blessing in the family. The question is where was Reuben did he see and hear the conversation between the two women and as well understand the situation that was unfolding before him. I truly believe that there were more instances that came about as these women fight for the attention of Jacob and looking toward the physical instead of searching for God in the times of trouble. In this was the aftermath of the developing of the character of Reuben. We can see this in the developing of Reuben in a particular situation that cause Reuben to loose everything by an act that was totally out of order of God's mandates. But before that we can see the moving of growth in Reuben in one area particularly. Let see what the Bible says: And Jacob dwelt in the land wherein his father was a stranger, in the land of Canaan. These are the generations of Jacob. Joseph, being seventeen years old, was feeding the flock with his brethren: and the lad was with the sons of Bil'-hah, and with the sons of Zil—pah, his father's wives: and Joseph brought unto his father their evil report.

Now Israel loved Joseph more than all his children, because he was the son of his old age: and he made him a coat of many colours. And when his brethren saw that their father loved him more than all his brethren, they hated him, and could not speak peaceably unto him. And Joseph dreamed a dream, and he told it his brethren: and they hated him ye the more. And he said unto them, Hear, I pray you, this dream which I have dreamed: For, behold, we were binding sheaves in the field, and, lo, my sheaf arose, and also stood upright; and, behold, your sheaves stood round about, and made obeisance to my sheaf. And his brethren said to him, Shalt thou indeed reign over us? or shalt thou indeed have dominion over us? And they hated him yet the more for his dreams, and for his words.

And he dreamed yet another dream, and told it his brethren, and said, Behold, I have dreamed a dream more; and, behold, the sun and the moon and the eleven stars made obeisance to me. And he told it to his father, and to his brethren: and his father rebuke him, and said unto him, What is this dream that thou hast dreamed? Shall I and thy mother and thy brethren indeed come to bow down ourselves to thee to the earth? And his brethren envied him; but his father observed the saying. And his brethren went to feed their father's flock in She'-chem. And Israel said unto Joseph, Do not thy brethren feed the flock in She'-chem? come, and I will send thee unto them. And he said to him, Here am I. And he said to him, Go, I pray thee, see whether it be well with thy brethren, and well with the flocks; and bring me word again. So he sent him out of the vale of He'-bron, and he came to She'-chem. And a certain man found him, and, behold, he was wandering in the field: and the man asked him, saying, What seekest thou? And he said, I seek my brethren: tell me, I pray thee, where they feed their flocks. And the man said, They are departed hence; for I heard them say, Let us go to Do'-than. And when they saw him afar off, even before he came near unto them, they conspired against him to slay him.

And they said one to another, Behold, this dreamer cometh. Come now therefore, and let us slay him, and cast him into some pit, and we will say, Some evil beast hath devoured him: and we shall see what will become of his dreams. And Reuben heard it, and he delivered him out of their hands; and said, Let us not kill him. And Reuben said unto them, Shed no blood, but cast him into this pit that is in the wilderness, and lay no hand upon him; that he might rid him out of their hands, to deliver him to his father again. And it came to pass, when Joseph was come unto his brethren, that they stript Joseph out of his coat, his coat of many colours that was on him; And they took him, and cast him into a pit: and the pit was empty, there was no water in it. And they sat down to eat bread: and they lifted up their eyes and looked, and behold, a company of Ish'-me-el-ites came from Gil'-e-ad wit their camels bearing spicery and balm and myrrh, going to carry it down to Egypt.

And Judah said unto his brethren, What profit is it if we slay our brother, and conceal his blood? Come, and let us sell him to the Ish'-me-el-ites, and let not our hand be upon him; for he is our brother and our flesh. And his brethren were content. Then there passed by Mid'-i-an-ites merchantmen; and they drew and lifted up Joseph out of the pit, and sold Joseph to the Ish'-me-el-ites for twenty pieces of silver: and they brought Joseph into Egypt. And Reuben returned unto the pit; and, behold, Joseph was not in the pit; and he rent his clothes. And he returned unto his brethren, and said, The child is not; and I whither shall I go? And they took Joseph's coat and killed a kid of the goats, and dipped the coat in the blood; And they sent the coat of many colours, and they brought it to their father; and said, This have we found: know now whether it be thy son's coat or no. And he knew it, and said, It is my son's coat; an evil beast hath devoured him; Joseph is without doubt rent in pieces. And Jacob rent his clothes, and put sackcloth upon his loins, and mourned for his son many days. And all his sons and all his daughters rose up to comfort him; but he refused to be comforted; and he said, For I will go down Into the grave unto my son mourning. Thus his father wept for him. And the Mid-i-an-ites sold him into Egypt unto Pot'-i-phar, an officer of Pharaoh's and captain of the guard. (Genesis 37: 1-36)

We see in chapter 37 of Genesis that Reuben compassion is developing slowly because he spoke up to his brethren about Joseph. He wanted to come back and release him but the brothers had already done the deed forewhich they come to realize was best for them. But what they did not know that they were the instruments that God used in the midst of their envy to fulfill the wishes of God for the life of Joseph. That in the fullness of time Joseph was in the right place at the right time to do the right thing for the right reason and brought fullness to Israel. But Reuben steady dealing with issues from child birth and deception and other devices moving in his life cause an action to come forth that move him from who he was supposed to me. Let us look at this: the Bible says: And it came to pass, when Israel dwelt in that land, that Reuben went and lay with Bil'-hah his father's concubine: and Israel heard it. Now the sons of Jacob were twelve: The sons of Leah; Reuben, Jacob's first born, and Simeon, and Levi, and Judah, and Is'-sa-char, and Zeb'-u-lun; The sons of Ra'-chel; Joseph and Benjamin: And the sons of Bil'-hah, Ra'-chel's handmaid; Dan, and Naph'-ta-li: And the sons of Zil'-pah, Leah's handmaid; Gad and Asher: these are the sons of Jacob, which were born to him in Padan-a'-ram. (Genesis 35: 22-26)

The Bible says also: If a man have two wives, one beloved, and another hated, and they have born him children, both the beloved and the hated: and if the firstborn son be hers that was hated: Then it shall be, when he maketh his sons to inherit that which he hath, that he may not make the son of the beloved firstborn before the son of the hated, which is indeed the firstborn: But he shall acknowledge the son of the hated for the firstborn, by giving him a double portion of all that the hath: for he is the beginning of his strength; the right of the firstborn is his. (Deuteronomy 21: 15-17) In this because of the act that Reuben committed by sleeping with his father's concubine he lost the rights given unto him as the firstborn. But in that trauma of the situation the movement of God was at hand simply because we saw the growth that moved Reuben to speak up to assist his brother from harm something was happening to Reuben on the inside. From the beginning we see the situation and circumstances forewhich he was born into that he carried unto himself that attached itself to him like a plague.

But within Reuben there begin to be a change that brought about a since of compassion forewhich he did not see early in his childhood but we know start coming into affect because of the maturity level of his mother growing in the acceptance of God's will in her life. In this we can say was being passed upon Reuben but remember there was so other stuff there that it took time to penetrate through the mess so the transformation could take place to produce a productive product. This evidence is clearer in the offspring of Reuben: the Bible says: And the sons of Reuben; Ha'-noch, and Phal'-lu, and Hez'-ron and Car'-mi. (Genesis 46:9) Hanoch means: dedicated for which he was the father of Hanochites. Hezron means: enclosure and he was the father of the Hezronites. Now on these two particular tribes we can spend sometime but for the sake of time we will move on.

Now let us look at compassion, which means: "deep sympathy" this definition gives great revelation. Let us break down this definition to better grasps the reality of this word. The word: "deep" means: adj. [[OE deop]] 1. extending far downward, inward, backward, etc. 2. hard to understand; abstruse 3. serious; profound 4. dark and rich [a deep thought] 6. great in degree; intense 7. of low pitch [a deep voice] 8. large; big –n a deep place – adv. far down, far back, etc. –the deep [Old Poet.] the ocean –deep'ly adv. –deep'ness n. (Webster's New World Dictionary) The word: "sympathy" means: n., pl –thies [[< Gr syn-, together + pathos, feeling]] 1. sameness of feeling 2. mutual liking or understanding 3. a) ability to share another's ideas, emotions, etc. b) pity or compassion for another's trouble or suffering. (Webster's New World Dictionary) Now let us put these two definitions together that will reveal the awesomeness of the meaning of compassion. The word compassion simply means: "extending far inward ability to share another's ideas, emotions, etc."

Now within this definition for compassion: "extending far inward ability to share another's ideas, emotions, etc." it gives off the true essence of understanding as well as being open to the pain and suffering forewhich another is going through. This reveals great revelation to our Lord Jesus

Christ in His great understanding regardless of how we felt about it knew the will of the Father. And in that felt the pain forewhich the Father felt in watching His children, His creation separated from Him. So Christ Himself found it not with strife or envy. "But made himself of no reputation, and took upon him the form of a servant, and was made in the likeness of men: And being found in fashion as a man, he humbled himself, and became obedient unto death, even the death of the cross." (Philippians 2:7-9) Now remember that in Christ was the compete transformation in mind, heart, body and soul together forewhich He wants us to be. But within our human form we have to work to get better in each area daily that brings us closer to the fashion of Christ.

We have to be willing to grow in these areas that will start a transformation within each area and release exactly what God needs in us to fulfill the will of God. This position we reach is the ability to understand and be able to feel the pain and understand the emotional trauma forewhich the adversary stirred up in them in situations and events that caused them to be pulled off of the mark forewhich God has sent up in their lives. Remember compassion means: "extending far inward ability to share another's ideas, emotions, etc." and we have a lot of obstacle as well as issues to deal with in order to reach this level of compassion. But in the pursuit of this is the evidence that gives power as well as recognition to God at all times and in everything we do. This is the key to the revelation of compassion especially within the growing of Reuben and his life. Did you see the compassion when he spoke up about his brother and did not want him kill and in his speaking up had intention to come back and get him and deliver him to the father.

Look at the compassion here about Reuben between him and his father in an act that neither fully understood but Reuben's growth had over come the obstacles that the adversary has place in his life. The Bible says: And they came unto Jacob their father unto the land of Canaan, and told him all that befell unto them; saying, The man who is the lord of the land, spake roughly to s, and took us for spies of the country. And we said unto him, We are true men; we are no spies: We be twelve brethren, sons of our father; one is not, and the youngest is this day with our father in the land Canaan. And the man, the lord of the country, said unto us, Hereby shall I know that ye are true men; leave one of your brethren here with me, and take food for the famine of your households, and be gone: And bring your youngest brother unto me: then shall I know that ye are no spies, but that ye are true men: so will I deliver you your brother, and ye shall traffick in the land. And it came to pass as they emptied their sacks, that, behold, every man's bundle of money was in his sack: and when both they and their father saw the bundles of money they were afraid. And Jacob their father said unto them, Me have ye bereaved of my children: Joseph is not, and Simeon is not, and ye will take Benjamin away: all these things are against me. And Reuben spake unto his father, saying, Slay my two sons, if I bring him not to thee: deliver him into my hand, and I will bring him to thee again. And he said, My son shall not go down with you; for his brother is dead, and he is left alone: if mischief befall him by the way in the which ye go, then shall ye bring down my gray hairs with sorrow to the grave. (Genesis 42: 29-38)

We see here that Reuben offered his own sons to replace the one's that was lost if he don't return with his brethren Simeon if Israel let Benjamin to go with them back to the lord of that land. Now what they did not know that it was Joseph and was Reuben filled with grief because of the lost of Joseph and the part he played in it as well as not releasing the information he knew about the entire situation. Or simply because he was not there when Joseph was sold and really did not know that the brothers did what they did was the situation that he saw every day on the face of Israel. Did he feel the pain of loosing a son forewhich he never lost one at that point, but could he feel it in the words and the situation from Israel. Compassion growing within Reuben was overwhelming the penetration of the adversary illusion pressing against the things that Reuben had done in his life God used it to create a character forewhich you and I need regardless of what we have been through.

You see within Reuben journey compassion was probably with him as he watches his mother suffer for the attention of Jacob. As well as he watches his mother grow within the area forewhich she was suffering in. Then we see how he went through justice without compassion in accordance to the great sin he committed with his father's concubine. The Bible says: Now the sons of Reuben the firstborn of Israel, (for he was the firstborn; but, forasmuch as he defiled his father's bed, his birthright was given unto the sons of Joseph the son of Israel: and the genealogy is not to be reckoned after the birthright. (1Chronicles 5:1) I want you to know that all these events within the life of Reuben was used for the good of the developing of the character of Reuben by way of growing from the mistakes made. As well as to see that regardless of what we have done within the plan of God we are able to get on target by the blood of Christ. This is very important as well, let me show you something.

Every tribe had a stone that represented the tribe that was on the Breast Plate of Righteousness forewhich the high priest wore. Now this is a subject we can spend a great deal on but just follow me as I reveal something to you. Now let us talk a little about the stone that represented the Tribe of Reuben. The Bible says: After this I looked, and, behold, a door was opened in heaven: and the first voice which I heard was as it were of a trumpet talking with me; which said, Come hither, and I will shew thee things which must be hereafter. And immediately I was in the spirit: and, behold, a throne was set in heaven, and one sat on the throne. And he that sat was to look upon like jasper and a sardine stone: and there was a rainbow round about the throne in sight like unto an emerald. And round about the throne were four and twenty seats: and upon the seats I saw four and twenty elders sitting, clothed in white raiment; and they had on their heads crowns of gold. (Revelation 4:1-4)

Carnelian is a precious stone of blood-red color that during Bible History was sometimes called "Sardine stone," or "sardius" because in ancient time it was obtained from Sardis in Asia Minor (Sardis was also the location of one of the prophetic Seven Churches of Revelation). As described in the verses above Sardine stone/carnelian is found at God's Throne in heaven while God's Throne remains in heaven; from Heaven to Earth. It also was chosen by God as one of the precious stones in Aaron's high-priest breastplate, as well as in the foundation of the New Jerusalem. Notice above how the key of the revelation for greater understanding comes jumping out as we see a word that illuminates the essence of the true nature of the power of the character. The word I am referring to is "Foundation" this word gives powerful understanding of the necessity of the gathering of the revelation unto our spiritual being because that will trigger a physical and mental reaction that secures a disposition of realism of the presence of God in ones life.

We as friends of the most high truly understand the foundation of the church, which is Christ Jesus. Look at the greater gathering in how the Apostle Luke uses an extra measure of the presence of God in his life being inspired by the spirit of God to write about the very thing that you and I can relate to. That is the Man Christ Jesus, which represents the mind of each of us through the spiritual intervention of Biblical Revelation of God's movement in our lives. This is very important to understand because God called us for some the road is this way or that way and for others it seems to be very out of whack for a while until the fullness of God's revelation is grasped do to the fact that the very essence of their fullness is to truly receive that God chose them. And regardless whether they want they must truly come to the realization it is not about them but the foundation that called them is the very foundation that must be built in them. Remember my friends that God has some within the body whom are a foundation for the edifying of the true wonders of the Lord!

Within this we see that compassion pivots around a central mechanism that propels the true essence of the revelation of God in one's life without the very essence of one even knowing it. In that we have to continue with the understanding of why one is chosen to certain things within the Body of Christ. This might sound funny to some but we as members of the Body of Christ our roles are different in nature but the same spiritually. In that we see that each role is important and each of us needs to fulfill our destiny in Christ Jesus. It always puzzle me about the area forewhich I was chosen to do within the Body of Christ. And until I come to the fullness of acceptance of my calling then I was not effective as I was called to be. And until I found this verse I never really understood it or fully embrace my calling. Let me share it with you, the Bible says: And the Lord said, Shall I hide from Abraham that thing which I do; Seeing that Abraham shall surely become a great and mighty nation, and all the nations of the earth shall be blessed in him? For I know him, that he will command his children and his household after him, and they shall keep the way of the Lord, to do justice and judgment; that the Lord may bring upon Abraham that which he hath spoken of him. (Genesis 18: 17-19) I want you to focus on a particular part of those verses or scriptures: For I know him, that he will command his children and his household after him, and they shall keep the way of the Lord, to do justice and judgment; that the Lord may bring upon Abraham that which he hath spoken of him. (Genesis 18: 19) I going to let that soak in your spirit for a while before we look a little deeper into that so let us move on to the Tribe of Reuben.

The Tribe of Reuben

I wanted to focus on the Tribe of Reuben for us to see the fulfilling of the calling forewhich God has called Reuben to be. But what we have to remember friends that we have to get where we need to be in order for those that follow us to come into the fullness of what they are called to be without going through the molding transformation of trials and tribulations. You see you can bring down the revelation of God into those that are around you that can set them free before they get caught up in the adversary delusions and penetrations. In this they reach the goal in the time frame forewhich God has called them to be in. Now remember it is God's timing for everything but we can move ourselves out of the time frame of God and the protection of God by moving in the time frame of the adversary. In this we see that we have to come to the realization of the revelation of God and start implementing the word of God in our lives that will draw us nearer to God and God appears to come closer to us. This simply means that our spiritual eye is open and we can see God clearer in our lives instead of seeing the confusion of the adversary presented in our sight because we are blinded to the will of God. Now let us prepare to follow the movement of the developing of the character of Reuben.

During 420 years in Egypt, the descendants of Reuben increased from four sons to 46,500 men of war. Notice that the prophecy of Jacob held fast only in Reuben spiritually but was not physically as the fullness of God took hold and multiplied the descendants of Reuben. Let us look at the prophecy of Reuben first. The Bible says: And Jacob called unto his sons, and said, Gather yourselves together, that I may tell you that which shall befall you in the last days. Gather yourselves together, and hear, ye sons of Jacob; and hearken unto Israel your father. Reuben, thou art my firstborn, my might, and the beginning of my strength, the excellency of dignity, and the excellency of power: Unstable as water, thou shalt not excel; because thou wentest up to thy father's bed; then defiledst thou it: he went up to my couch. (Genesis 49:1-4)

That prophecy is from Israel the father of Reuben that places him in the position forewhich he was supposed to be but lost it by a great sin. Jacob also indicated that Reuben was unstable as if to say emotionally or psychologically and spiritually unsettled. But we see that these areas grown in Reuben and extended toward the tribe in the blessing of Moses. The Bible says: And this is the blessing, wherewith Moses the man of God blessed the children of Israel before his death. And he said, The Lord came from Si'-nai, and rose up from Se'-ir unto them; he shined forth from mount Pa'-ran, and he came with ten thousands of saints: from his right hand went a fiery law for them. Yea, he loved the people; all his saints are in thy hand: and they sat down at thy feet; every one shall receive of thy words. Moses commanded us a law, even the inheritance of the congregation of Jacob. And he was king in Jesh'-u-run, when the heads of the people and the tribes of Israel were gathered together. Let Reuben live, and not die; and let not his men be few. (Deuteronomy 33: 1-6)

We see here in Moses prophecy the spoke to Moses to tell the descendants of Reuben to live and not die and let them multiply. And we see in the numbers that we counted in Egypt proved from four sons grew to 46,500 and we can say what an increase that is directly linked to the growth of the spiritual connection of their father that took him from unstable, emotionally, psychologically and spiritually unsettled to becoming a nation that is to live and multiply. This gives great revelation unto you and I to see that the power of the foundation of the calling carries the weight to the transformation by way of renewing the mind and transforming the heart that illuminates the very essence or foundation of Christ. Now within the movement of the tribe there still was growth that was needed and they went through different trials and tribulations that caused there own particular set of situations. Let us take a look at some of the situations and circumstances.

In the wilderness the Tribe of Reuben was represented in a conspiracy against Moses. Using the law by being the descendants of the oldest son they wanted to be the leaders of Israel. This is interesting because in their history they know that their father lost his right to the birthright of being leader and double portion and it was the growing in faith and knowledge of God brought forth the mercy of God. But let us take a look at this. The Bible says: Now Ko'-rah, the son of Iz'-har, the son of Ko'-hath, the son of Levi, and Da'-than and A-bi'-ram, the sons of E-li'-ab, and On, the son of Pe'-leth sons of Reuben, took men: And they rose up before Moses, with certain of the children of Israel, two hundred and fifty princes of the assembly, famous in the congregation, men of renown: And they gathered themselves together against Moses and against Aaron, and said unto them, Ye take too much upon you, seeing all the congregation are holy, every one of them and the Lord is among them: wherefore then lift ye up yourselves above the congregation of the Lord? And when Moses heard it, he fell upon his face: And he spake unto Ko'-rah and unto all his company, saying, even to morrow the Lord will shew who are his, and who is holy; and will cause him to come near unto him: even him whom he hath chosen will he cause to come near unto him.

This do; Take you censers, Ko'-rah, and all his company; And put fire therein, and put incense in them before the Lord to morrow: and it shall be that the man whom the Lord doth choose, he shall be holy: ye take too much upon you, ye sons of Levi. And Moses said unto Ko'-rah, Hear, I pray you, ye sons of Levi: Seemeth it but a small thing unto you, that the God of Israel hath separated you from the congregation of Israel, to bring you near to himself to do the service of the tabernacle of the Lord, and to stand before the congregation to minister unto them? And he hath brought thee near to him, and all thy brethren the sons of Levi with thee: and seek ye the priesthood also? For which cause both thou and II thy company are gathered together against the Lord: and what is Aaron that ye murmur against him? And Moses set to call Da'-than and A-bi'-ram the sons of E-li'-ab: which said, We will not come up: It is a small thing that thou hast brought us up out of a land that floweth with milk and honey, to kill us in the wilderness, except thou make thyself altogether a prince over us? Moreover thou hast not brought us into a land that floweth with milk and honey, or given us inheritance of fields and vineyards: wilt thou put out the eyes of these men? we will not come up.

And Moses said unto Ko'-rah, Be thou and all thy company before the Lord, thou, and they, and Aaron, to morrow: And take every man his censer, and put incense in them and bring ye before the Lord every man his censer, two hundred and fifty censers; thou also and Aaron each of you his censer. And they took every man his censer, and put fire in them, and laid incense thereon, and stood in the door of the tabernacle of the congregation with Moses and Aaron. And Ko'-rah gathered all the congregation against them unto the door of the tabernacle of the congregation: and the glory of the Lord appeared unto al the congregation. And the Lord spake unto Moses and unto Aaron, saying, Separate yourselves from among this congregation, that I may consume them in a moment. And they fell upon their faces and said, O God, the God of the spirits of all flesh, shall one man sin, and wilt thou be wroth with all the congregation? And the Lord spake unto Moses, saying, Speak unto the congregation, saying, Get you up from about the tabernacle of Ko'-rah, Da'-than and A-bi'-ram; and the elders of Israel followed him.

And he spake unto the congregation, saying, Depart, I pray you, from the tents of these wicked men, and touch nothing of theirs, lest ye be consumed in all their sins. So they gat up from the tabernacle of Ko'-rah, Da'-than, and A-bi'-ram, on every side: and Da'-than and A-bi'-ram came out, and stood in the door of their tents, and their wives, and their sons, and their little children. And Moses said, Hereby ye shall know that the Lord hath sent me to do all these works; for I have not done them of mine own mind. If these men die the common death of all men, or if they be visited after the visitation of all men; then the Lord hath not sent me. But if the Lord make a new thing, and the earth open her mouth, and swallow them up, with all that appertain unto them, and they go down quick into the pit; then ye shall understand that these men have provoked the Lord. And it came to pass, as he had made an end of speaking all these words, that the ground clave asunder that was under them: And the earth opened her mouth, and swallowed them up, and their houses, and all the men that appertained unto Ko'-rah, and all their goods.

They, and all that appertained to them, went down alive into the pit, and the earth closed upon them: and they perished from among the congregation. And all Israel that were around about them fled at the cry of them: for they said, Lest the earth swallow us up also. And there came out a fire from the Lord, and consumed the two hundred and fifty men that offered incense. And the Lord spake unto Moses, saying, Speak unto E-le-a'-zar the son of Aaron the priest, that the take up the censers out of the burning, and scatter thou the fire yonder; for they are hallowed. The censers of these sinners against their own souls, let them make them broad plates for a covering of the altar: for they offered them before the Lord, therefore they are hallowed: and they shall be a sign unto the children of Israel. And E-le-a'-zar the priest took the brazen censers, wherewith they that were burnt had offered; and they were made broad plates for a covering of the altar: To be a memorial unto the children of Israel, that no stranger, which is not of the seed of Aaron, come near to offer incense before the Lord; that he be not as Ko'-rah, and as his company: as the Lord said to him by the hand of Moses.

But on the morrow all the congregation of the children of Israel murmured against Moses and against Aaron, saying, Ye have killed the people of the Lord. And it came to pass, when the congregation was gathered against Moses and against Aaron, that they looked toward the tabernacle of the congregation: and behold, the cloud covered it, and the glory of the Lord appeared. And the Lord spake unto Moses, saying, Get you up from among this congregation, that I may consume them as in a moment, And they fell upon their faces. And Moses said unto Aaron, Take censer, and put fire therein from off the altar, and put on incense, and go quickly unto the congregation and make an atonement for them: for there is wrath gone out from the Lord; the plague is begun. And Aaron took as Moses commanded, and ran into the midst of the congregation; and, behold, the plague was begun among the people: and he put on incense, and made an atonement for the people. And he stood between the dead and the living; and the plague was stayed. Now they that died in the plague were fourteen thousand and seven hundred, beside them that died about the matter of Ko'-rah. And Aaron returned unto Moses unto the door of the tabernacle of the congregation: and the plague was stayed.

And the Lord spake unto Moses, saying, Speak unto the children of Israel, and take of every one of them a rod according to the house of their fathers, of all their princes according to the house of their fathers twelve rods: write thou every man's name upon his rod. And thou shalt write Aaron's name upon the rod of Levi: for one rod shall be for the head of the house of their fathers. And thou shalt lay them up in the tabernacle of the congregation before the testimony, where I will meet with you. And it came to pass, that the man's rod, whom I shall choose, shall blossom: I will make to cease from me the murmurings of the children of Israel, whereby thy murmur against you. And Moses spake unto the children of Israel, every one of their princes gave his a rod apiece for each prince one, according to their father's houses even twelve rods: and the rod of Aaron was among their rods. And Moses laid up the rods before the Lord in the tabernacle of witness. And it came to pass that on the morrow Moses went into the tabernacle of witness; and, behold, the rod of Aaron for the house of Levi was budded, and brought forth buds, and bloomed blossoms, and yielded almonds.

And Moses brought out all the rods from before the Lord unto all the children of Israel: and they looked, and took every man his rod. And the Lord said unto Moses, Bring Aaron's rod again before the testimony, to be kept for a token against the rebels; and thou shalt quite take away their murmurings from me, that they die not. And Moses did so: as the Lord commanded him, so did he. And the children of Israel spake unto Moses, saying, Behold, we die, we perish, we all perish. Whosoever cometh any thing near unto the tabernacle of the Lord shall die: shall we be consumed with dying? (Numbers 16-17) Within the movement of the Tribe of Reuben there was still holding on to the principle of man and refuse to grasps the reality of God's mandates that holds supreme over man's principle. In this Korah was able to insight them by the penetration of emotional instability that cause the destruction of that particular seed. As well here is a thought that in the plagued that caused over 14,000 deaths how many of them were from the house of Reuben. This presents another area forewhich God was removing all doubt out of the tribe of Reuben that secured their position in the Body of Christ.

In this an awesome revelation comes forth that we as members of the Body of Christ have to realize that we draw from our mistakes and grow from them and if not we are setting ourselves up for a destruction that can be quick and cost dearly. Notice that after the aftermath that Aaron rod was the one that budded as well as bear fruit. This gives us evidence that within the will of God or the plan of God we become fruitful or produce an effective product once we are in the position we are suppose to be. In this is the secret to the movement of the Tribe of Reuben trials and tribulations. Just as it is a blueprint for you and I to gain understanding and strength from to see ourselves clearer in the will and plan of God. In the essence of the word of God is a well laid plan that God is placing us within the scheme of things and we have to be willing to submit ourselves to the will of God that gives us assurance of being that productive member of the Body of Christ that produces an effective product to edify and glorify the Body of Christ.

We need to be so secure in our path that another with a good sounding idea can not move us out of our destiny just as Korah took hold of the past of Reuben and caused a destruction that was even passed downward upon the families which stood against God's chosen. We as members of the Body of Christ has to come to the understanding that Christ defeated our adversary and rose with all power in that He became the wholly sacrifice of God that took the penalty of sin from us and gave us a door out of the wrath of God. But in that we are still responsible for our actions and our actions carries weight not only in the physical but also in the spiritual. Sins of the father do not carry on to the son but the seed planted in that sin does. This is where the need to constantly look at ourselves and address the issues we have and filter them through the word of God to release the generational plagues of our house. In this we have to realize that God's plan is the ultimate plan and we are the tools used forewhich He loved so much gave us evidence of His love by creating a door for us to escape. In that escape is the freeing of the baggage carried by us that is in our character make up that holds the seed of the destruction forewhich the adversary uses against us.

But if we stay in the word of God the revelation of that seed will appear and then you and I can address that area by implementing the principles of God that transforms us by the renewing of the mind and the transformation of the heart that pushes outward that gives unmistakable evidence that it is Christ that have done this in your life. We see in the Tribe of Reuben that we can see that it was God moving in their lives to transform the penetration of the adversary to prune away the seed that was unfruitful and started and growing process of maturing in the will of God. Here is the key to the revelation that God uses different situations and circumstances that removes certain hidden penetrations of the adversary as well as passed along seed that is not productive to cause and growing in the maturity of the will of God. This is why the embracing of the process is so important simply because we know that when we are going through God is moving in our favor to prune us in away that we become a productive product to edify the Body of Christ and glorify God. Regardless of the situation the Tribe of Reuben was growing in the ways of spiritual maturity that was forcing them into the level which God needed them to be in to use them in away that you and I can see ourselves in. This is very interesting simply for you and I we have one that came from the heavens above and set our course engraved in the wounds of His hands. Now I want to reveal something to you that I want you to hold on to in your spirit. The word "Reuben" means: "Behold a son" this is very interesting and we are not going to get into that right now but just hold on to that. Let us continue onward with the Tribe of Reuben developing.

The tribe moved into the promise land as pastoral people shepherds of cattle and they saw the place that was suitable for cattle. So they requested early inheritance east of the Jordan River. They also helped the other tribes claim their land, and it was very interesting how Joshua recognize them. The Bible says: Then Joshua called the Reu'-ben-ites, and the Gad'-ites, and the half tribe of Ma-nas'-seh, And said unto them, Ye have kept all that Moses the servant of the Lord commanded you, and have obeyed my voice in all that it commanded you: Ye have not left your brethren these many days unto this day, but have kept the charge of the commandment of the Lord your God. And now the Lord your God hath given rest unto your brethren, as he promised them: therefore now return ye, and get you unto your tents, and unto the land of your possession which Moses the servant of the Lord gave you on the other side Jordan. But take diligent heed to do the commandment and the law, which Moses the servant of the Lord charged you, to love the Lord your God, and to walk in all his ways, and to keep his commandments, and to cleave unto him, and to serve him with all your heart and with all your soul.

So Joshua blessed them, and sent them away: and they went unto their tents. Now to the one half of the tribe of Ma-nas'-seh Moses had given possession n Ba'-shan: but unto the other half thereof gave Joshua among their brethren on this side Jordan westward. And when Joshua sent them away also unto their tents, then he blessed them. And he spake unto them, saying, Return with much riches unto your tents, and with very much cattle, with silver, and with gold, and with brass, and with iron, and with very much raiment: divide the spoil of your enemies with your brethren. And the children of Reuben and the children of God and the half tribe of Ma-nas'-seh returned and departed from the children of Israel to of Shi'-loh, which is in the land of Canaan, to go unto the country of Gil'-e-ad, to the land of their possession, whereof they were possessed, according to the word of he Lord by the hand of Moses. And when they came unto the borders of Jordan, that are in the land of Canaan, the children of Reuben and the children of God and the half tribe of Ma-nas'-seh built altar to see to. (Joshua: 22:1-10)

Notice how the maturity level of the Reubenites had grown to the point that Joshua commended them on following the commandments of the Lord their God. And he blessed them, which releases a great revelation for you and I. Regardless of our past and the journey it took for us to get where we are today even thou there are something that are with us remind us of the past deeds that we have done, God arms are wide open to receive us as we grow in Him through the knowledge of Jesus Christ. Once the Tribe of Reuben started to obey the word of God and God's mandates then we can see that the healing process begin and the developing of the character of Reubenites moved toward the calling forewhich the Lord had called them to be. We see that the journey forewhich they were on took them through a many obstacles and a many traps of the adversary but through obedience they became into the fullness of their character. This gives us the true essence of the word of God of showing us how obedience is better than sacrifice simply because in obedience we have to make a choice to follow which also incorporates sacrifice.

You have to get this that within the Tribe of Reuben they made some choices that cost them dearly but once they learn to release what they wanted and how they wanted to do things and start obeying God then they move from where they want to what God wanted for them. They were not immune to the attacks of the adversary at this time but the attacks had know effect on their spiritual growth simply because they released their emotions and psychological that was unstable and secured it the word and mandates of God. So the attacks had know effect on them and as they renewed their mind and their hearts was being transformed into the servitude of God then they start releasing something that not only was seen by them but others recognize the transformation as well. Simply because Joshua called unto them and told them they were doing what God told them to do. Notice the change from unstable to stable from four to over forty thousand from self-centerness to open and compassionate toward the hearing and moving in the word of God. This did not happen all in one day or one week or one year simply because it took a start and a feeding and a desire that took the garbage out of their lives and brought forth a productive product that was edifying to the Body of Christ and glorified God.

This does not mean that they were perfect in all their actions but they were moving in the actions of the Lord that transformed them. They still made mistakes as well made some stands that others thought was wrong but they stood by them. Interesting how God can tell you to do something and it seems so overwhelming that you think you need this person and that person and this thing and that thing but God told you just to take this and this person. But the overwhelming odds against you that you want more simply because it was in your power to get more, this happen in the instance between Deborah and Barak forewhich some miss the mighty revelation in this particular situation. Israel is now being called again to the righteousness of God and within the situation Deborah and Barak being called by God to perform the will God is standing in the gap for the children of Israel as they do evil in the sight of the Lord. But within this situation I want you to see the position of the Reubenites.

The Bible says: So God subdued on that day Ja'-bin the king of Canaan before the children of Israel. And the hand of the children of Israel prospered, and prevailed against Ja'-bin the king of Canaan, until they had destroyed Ja'-bin king of Canaan. Then sang Deb'-o-rah and Ba'-rak the son of A-bin'-o-am on that day, saying, Praise ye the Lord for the avenging of Israel, when the people willingly offered themselves. Hear, O ye kings: give ear, o ye princes; I, even I, will sing unto the Lord; I will sing praise to the Lord God of Israel. Lord, when thou wentest out of Se'-ir, when thou marchest out of the field of E'-dom, the earth trembled, and the heavens dropped, the clouds also dropped water. The mountains melted from before the Lord, even that Is'-nai from before the Lord God of Israel. In the days of Sham'-gar the son of A'-nath, in the days of Ja'-el, the high ways were unoccupied, and the travelers walked through byways. The inhabitants of the villages ceased, they ceased in Israel, until that Deb'-o-rah arose, that I arose a mother in Israel. They chose new gods; then was war in the gates: was there a shield of spear seen among forty thousand in Israel?

My heart is toward the governors of Israel, that offered themselves willingly among the people. Bless ye the Lord. Speak, ye that ride on white asses, ye that sit in judgment, and walk by the way. They that are delivered from the noise of archers in the places of drawing water, there shall they rehearse the righteous acts of the Lord, even the righteous acts toward the inhabitants of his villages in Israel: then shall the people of the Lord go down to the gates. Awake, awake, Deb'-o-rah: awake, awake, utter a song: arise, Ba'-rak and lead thy captivity captive, thou son of A-bin'-o-am. Then he made him that remaineth have dominion over the nobles among the people: the Lord made me have dominion over the mighty. Out of E'-phra-im was there a root of them against Am'-a-lek: after thee, Benjamin, among thy people; out of Ma'-chir came down governors, and out of Zeb'-u-lun they that handle the pen of the writer. And the princes of Is'-sa-char, and also Ba'-rak: he was sent on foot into the valley. For the divisions of Reuben there were great thoughts of heart. Why abodest thou among the sheepfolds, to hear the bleatings of the flocks? For the division of Reuben there were great searching of heart. (Judges 4:23-24: 5:1-16)

Now I want you to get the fullness of this particular situation in the existence of the Reubenites, and in order to do that we have to look at Deborah for a moment. Deborah was the fifth judge of Israel, a prophetess and the only female judge. Deborah's home was in the hill country of Ephraim and was the wife of Lapidoth. She judged from a particular spot, which became a landmark and was known as "the palm tree of Deborah." The Bible says: And the children of Israel again did evil in the sight of the Lord, when E'-hud was dead. And the Lord sold them into the hand of Ja'-bin king of Canaan, that reigned in Ha'-zor; the captain of whose host was Sis'-e-ra, which dwelt in Ha-ro'-sheth of the Gentiles. And the children of Israel cried unto the Lord: for he had nine hundred chariots of iron; and twenty years he mightily oppressed the children of Israel. And Deb'-o-rah, a prophetess, the wife of Lap'-i-doth, she judged Israel at that time. And she dwelt under the palm tree of Deb'-o-rah between Ra'-mah and Beth'-el in mount E'-phra-im: and the children of Israel came up to her for judgment. (Judges 4: 1-5)

Deborah summoned Barak and told him it was God's will that he lead her forces against the mighty warrior, Sisera. Now when God planted this within Deborah he gave specific instruction who to take and how many to take and what would happen as she reached for battle against Sisera. The Bible says: And she sent and called Ba'-rak the son of A-bin'-o-am out of Ke'-desh-naph'-ta-li, and said unto him, Hath not the Lord God of Israel commanded, saying, Go and draw toward mount Ta'-bor, and take with thee ten thousand men of the children of Naph'-ta-li and of the children of Zeb'-u-lun? And I will draw unto thee to the river Ki'-shon, Sis'-e-ra, the captain of Ja'-bin's army with his chariots and his multitude; and I will deliver him into thine hand. (Judges 4:6-7) Barak accepted the summons on one condition that Deborah comes with him.

Deborah and Barak's army consisted of only 10,000 while Sisera had a multitude of fighters and 900 chariots of iron. However God was on Israel's side and when the battle ended not a single man of Sisera's army survived, except Sisera himself, who fled on foot. But the wrath of God was upon him as he took refuge in the tent of Heber the Kenite, Jael who was the wife of Heber drove a tent peg through his temple killing him. Now when Deborah and Barak went forth to fulfill the will of God look at the reaction of the Tribe of Reuben. The Bible says: And the princes of Is'-sa-char were with Deb'-o-rah; even Is'-sa-char, and also Ba'-rak: he was sent on foot into the valley. For the divisions of Reuben there were great thoughts of heart. Why abodest thou among the sheepfolds, to hear the bleatings of the flocks? For the divisions of Reuben there were great searchings of heart. (Judges 5:3) Now knowing that God did not call Reuben to be with Deborah and Barak was the will of God but it cause some searching of the heart of Reuben. Simply and most interesting that the tribe knew that their brethren was out numbered and who they were going into battle with had chariots as well so they were out gun,

Reubenites feelings for the brethren had grown to such a proportion that it was a miracle by itself. So in this we see that they submitted unto to the will of God, which brought forth victory for his brethren verses the overwhelming compassion of his own heart. This shows growth and maturity on the part of the Reubenites but also it shows you and I that everything that God does within the area forewhich we are experienced in He does not have to use us to get the job done. In other words we might be good organizers and we see some other situation or circumstance that could use our help. But these are not a situation or circumstance that God called you in to do. This might be a thing were God is developing another one's skilled in that area to prepare them for what is to come. Were if we intervene then the person would not come to develop in that area. Simply put we are more effective to the Kingdom of God if we are moving in the will of God and not running off of our emotions and feelings, and mental progressions.

If we sit and wait on the Lord to move us and guide us into the path forewhich He has laid out for us then we become that vessel which can be used to produce and more effective product to advance and edify the Body of Christ and glorify God. In this we are being obedient to the will of God and bringing under submission emotionally, psychologically, as well as physically that brings the pure essence of the awesomeness of God. This also shows more Christ than anything else. You see having compassion is great and spiritual gifts are wonderful but if you are not able to bring that under the will of God to move in His season and His time then the gift is becoming a hindrance to you and the Body of Christ. But when that gift is surrendered to the will of God then the true essence of God's will is portrayed and the true foundation of Jesus Christ is pushed outwardly among us.

Now the Reubenites also encountered a situation that was so tremendous in deed and raised the very essence of the compassion for one over brethren that explodes the true essence of the very mission of Jesus Christ. I am so moved by this that I don't want you to miss this that I am going to put this situation here for you and I to receive the fullness of the word of God. The Bibles says: And it came to pass in those days, when there was no king in Israel, that there was a certain Levite sojourning on the side of mount E'-phra-im, who took to him a concubine out of Beth'-le-hem-ju'-dah. And his concubine played the whore against him, and went away from him unto her father's house to Beth'-le-hem-ju'-dah, and was there four whole months. Sand her husband arose, and went after her, to speak friendly unto her, and to bring her again, having his servant with him, and a couple of asses: and she brought him into her father's house: and when the father of the damsel saw him, he rejoiced to meet him. And his father in law, the damsel's father, retained him; and he abode with him three days: so they did eat and drink, and lodged there. And it came to pass on the fourth day, when they arose early in the morning, that he rose up to depart: and the damsel's father said unto his son n law, Comfort thine heart with a morsel of bread, and afterward go your way. And they sat down and did eat and drink both of them together: for the damsel's father had said unto the man, Be content, I pray thee, and tarry all night, and let thine heart be merry.

And when the man rose up to depart, his father in law urged him: therefore he lodged there again. And he arose early in the morning on the fifth day to depart: and the damsel's father said, Comfort thine heart, I pray thee. And they tarried until afternoon, and they did eat both of them. And when the man rose up to depart, he and his concubine, and his servant, his father in law the damsel's father, said unto him Behold. Now the day draweth toward evening, I pray you tarry all night: behold, the day groweth to an end, lodge here, that thine heart may be merry; and to morrow get you early on your way, that thou mayest go home. But the man would not tarry that night, but he rose up and departed, and came over against Je'-bus, which is Jerusalem; and there were wit h him two asses saddled, his concubine also was with him. And when they were by Je'-bus, the day was far spend; and the servant said unto his master, Come, I pray thee, and let us turn in into this city of the Jeb'-u-sites, and lodge in it. And his master said unto him, We will not turn aside hither into the city of a stranger, that is not of the children of Israel; we will pass over to Gib'-e-ah.

And he said unto his servant, Come, and let us draw near to one of these places to lodge all night, in Gib'-e-ah, or in Ra'-mah. And they passed on and went their way; and the sun went down upon them when they were by Gid'-e-ah, which belongeth to Benjamin. And they turned aside thither, to go in and to lodge in Gib'-e-ah: and when he went in, he sat him down in a street of the city: for there was no man that took them into his house to lodging. And, behold, there came an old man from his work out of the mount E'-phra-im; and he sojourned in Gib'-e-ah: but the men of the place were Benjamites. And when he had lifted up his eyes, he saw a wayfaring man in the street of the city: and the old man said, Whither goest thou? and whence comest thou? And he said unto him, We are passing from Beth'-le-hem-ju'-dah, but I am now going to the house of the Lord; and there is no man that receiveth me to house. Yet there is both straw and provender for our asses; and there is bread and wine also for me, and for thy handmaid, and for the young man which is with thy servants: there is no want of any thing.

And the old man said, Peace be with thee; howsoever let all thy wants lie upon me; only lodge not in the street. So he brought him into his house, and gave provender unto the asses: and they washed their feet, and did eat and drink. Now as they were making their hearts merry, behold, the men of the city, certain sons of Be'-li-al, beset the house round about, and beat at the door, and spake to the master of the house, the old man, saying, Bring forth the man that came into thine house, that we may know him. And the man, the master of the house, went out unto them, and said unto them, Nay, my brethren, nay, I pray you, do not so wickedly; seeing that this man is come into mine house, do not this folly. Behold, here is my daughter a maiden, and his concubine; them I will bring out now, and humble ye them, and do with them what seemeth good unto you: but unto this man do not so vile a thing. But the men would not hearken to him: so the man took his concubine, and brought her forth unto them; and they knew her, and abused her all the night until the morning: and when the day began to spring, they let her go.

Then came the woman in the dawning of the day, and fell down at the door of the man's house where her lord was, till it was light. And her lord rose up in the morning, and opened the doors of the house, and went out to go his way: and, behold, the woman his concubine was fallen down at the door of the house, and her hands were upon the threshold. And he said unto her, Up, and let us be going. But none answered. Then the man took her up upon an ass, and the man rose up and gat him unto his place. And when he was come into the house, he took a knife, and laid hold on his concubine, and divided her, together with her bones into twelve pieces, and sent her into all the coasts of Israel. And it was so that all that saw it said, There was no such deed done nor seen from the day that the children of Israel came up out of the land of Egypt unto this day: consider of it, take advice and speak your minds.

Then all the children of Israel went out, and the congregation was gathered together as one man, from Dan even to Be'-er-she'-ba, with the land of Gil'-e-ad, unto the Lord in Miz'-peh. And the chief of all the people, even of all the tribes of Israel, presented themselves in the assembly of the people of God, four hundred thousand footmen that drew sword. (Now the children of Benjamin heard that the children of Israel were gone up to Miz'-peh.) Then said the children of Israel, Tell us, how was this wickedness? And the Levite, the husband of the woman that was slain, answered and said, I came into Gid'-e-ah that belongeth to Benjamin, I and my concubine, to lodge. And the men of Gid'-e-ah rose against me, and beset the house round about upon me by night, and thought to have slain me: and my concubine have they forced, that she is dead. And I took my concubine, and cut her in pieces, and sent her throughout all the country of the inheritance of Israel: for they have committed lewdness and folly in Israel. Behold, ye are all children of Israel; give here your advice and counsel.

And all the people arose as one man, saying, We will not any of us go to his tent , neither will we any of us turn into his house. But now this shall be the thing which we will do to Gib'-e-ah; we will go up by lot against it; And we will take tem men of an hundred throughout all the tribes of Israel, and an hundred of a thousand, and a thousand to o f ten thousand, to fetch victual for the people, that they may do, when they come to Gib'-e-ah of Benjamin, according to all the folly that they have wrought in Israel. So all the men of Israel were gathered against the city, knit together as one man. And the tribes of Israel sent men through all the tribe of Benjamin, saying, What wickedness is this that is done among you? Now therefore deliver us the men, the children of Be'-li-al, which are in Gib'-e-ah, that we may put them to death, and put away evil from Israel. But the children of Benjamin would not hearken to the voice of their brethren the children of Israel: But the children of Benjamin gathered themselves together out of the cities unto Gib'-e-ah, to go out to battle against the children of Israel.

And the children of Benjamin were numbered at that time out of the cities twenty and six thousand men that drew sword, beside the inhabitants of Gib'-e-ah, which were numbered seven hundred chosen men. Among all this people there were seven hundred chosen men lefthanded; every one could sling stones at an hair breadeth, and not miss. And the men of Israel, beside Benjamin, were numbered four hundred thousand men that drew sword: all these were men of war. And the children of Israel arose, and went up to the house of God, and asked counsel of God, and said, Which shall of us shall go up first to the battle against the children of Benjamin? And the Lord said, Judah shall go up first. And the children of Israel rose up in the morning, and encamped against Gib'-e-ah. And the men of Israel went out to battle against Benjamin; and the men of Israel put themselves in array to fight against them at Gib'-e-ah.

And the children of Benjamin came forth out of Gib'-e-ah, and destroyed down to the ground of the Israelites that day twenty and two thousand men. And the people the men of Israel encouraged themselves, and set their battle again in array in the place where they put themselves in array the first day. (And the children of Israel went up and wept before the Lord until even, and asked counsel of the Lord, saying, Shall I go up again to battle against the children of Benjamin my brother? And the Lord said, Go up against him.) And the children of Israel came near against the children of Benjamin the second day. And Benjamin went forth against them out of Gib'-e-ah the second day, and destroyed down to the ground of the children of Israel again eighteen thousand men; all these drew the sword. Then all the children of Israel, and all the people, went up, and came unto the house of God, and wept, and sat there before the Lord, and fasted that day until even, and offered burnt offerings and peace offerings before the Lord. And the children of Israel enquired of the Lord, (for the ark of the covenant of God was there in those days, And Phin'-e-has, the son of E-le-a'-zar, the son of Aaron, stood before it in those days,) saying, Shall I yet again go out to battle against the children of Benjamin my brother, or shall I cease? And the Lord said, Go up; for to morrow I will deliver them into thine hand.

And Israel set liers in wait round about Gid'-e-ah. And the children of Israel went up against the children of Benjamin on the third day, and put themselves in array against Gid-e-ah, as the other times. And the children of Benjamin went out against the people, and were drawn away from the city; and they began to smite of the people, and kill, as at other times, goeth up to the house of God, and the other to Gib'-e-ah in the field about thirty men of Israel. And the children of Benjamin said, They are smitten down before us, as at the first. But the children of Israel said, Let us flee, and draw them from the city unto the highways. And all the men of Israel rose up out of their place, and put themselves in array at Ba'-al-ta'-mar: and the liers in wait of Israel came forth out of their places, even out of the meadows of Gib'-e-ah. And there came against Gib'-e-ah ten thousand chosen men out of all Israel, and the battle was sore: but they knew not that evil was near them.

And the Lord smote Benjamin before Israel: and the children of Israel destroyed of the Benjamites that day twenty and five thousand and an hundred men: all these drew the sword. So the children of Benjamin saw that they were smitten: for the men of Israel gave place to the Benjamites, because they trusted unto the liers in wait which they had set beside Gid'-e-ah. And the liers in wait hasted, and rush upon Gib'-e-ah; and the liers in wait drew themselves along, and smote all the city with the edge of the sword. Now there was an appointed sign between the men of Israel and the liers in wait, that they should make a great flame with smoke rise up out of the city. And when the men of Israel retired in the battle, Benjamin began to smite and kill of the men of Israel about thirty persons: for they said, Surely they are smitten down before us, as in the first battle. But when the flame began to arise up out of the city with a pillar of smoke, the Benjamites looked behind them, and behold the flame of the city ascended up to heaven.

And when the men of Israel turned again, the men of Benjamin were amazed: for they saw that evil was come upon them. Therefore they turned their backs before the men of Israel unto the way of the wilderness; but the battle overtook them; and them which came out of the cities they destroyed in the midst of them. Thus they inclosed the Benjamites round about, and chased them, and trode them down with ease over against Gib'-e-ah toward the sunrising. And there fell there fell of Benjamin eighteen thousand men; all these were men of valour. And they turned and fled toward the wilderness unto the rock of Rim'-mon: and they gleaned of them in the highways five thousand men; and pursued hard after them unto Gi'-dom, and slew two thousand men of them. So that all which fell that day of Benjamin were twenty and five thousand men that drew the sword; all these were men of valour. But six hundred men turned and fled to the wilderness unto the rock Rim'-mon, and abode in the rock Rim'-mon, four months. And the men of Israel turned again upon the children of Benjamin, and smote them with the edge of the sword, as well the men of every city, as the beast, and all that came to hand: also they set on fire all the cities that they came to.

Now the men of Israel had sworn in Miz'-peh, saying, There shall not any of us give his daughter unto Benjamin to wife. And the people came to the house of God, and abode there till even before God, and lifted up their voices, and wept sore; And said, O Lord God of Israel, why is this come to pass in Israel, that there should be to day one tribe lacking in Israel? And it came to pass on the morrow that the people rose early, and built there an altar, and offered burnt offerings and peace offerings. And the children of Israel said, Who is there among all the tribes of Israel that came not up with the congregation unto the Lord? For they had made a great oath concerning him that came not up to the Lord to Miz'-peh, saying, He shall surely be put to death. And the children of Israel repented them for Benjamin their brother, and said, There is one tribe cut off from Israel this day. How shall we do for wives for them that remain, seeing we have sworn by the Lord that we will not give them of our daughters to wives? And they said, What one is there of the tribes of Israel that came not up to Miz-peh to the Lord? And, behold, there came none to the camp from Ja'-besh-gil'-e-ad to the assembly.

For the people were numbered, and behold there were none of the inhabitants of Ja'-besh-gil'-e-ad there. And the congregation sent thither twelve thousand men of the valiantest, and commanded them, saying, Go and smite the inhabitants of Ja-besh-gil'-e-ad with the edge of the sword, with the women and the children. And this is the thing that ye shall do, Ye shall utterly destroy every male, and every woman that hath lain by man. And they found among the inhabitants of Ja'-besh-gil'-e-ad four hundred young virgins, that had known no man by lying with any male: and they brought them unto the camp to Shi'-loh, which I sin the land of Canaan. And the whole congregation sent some to speak to the children of Benjamin that were in the rock Rim'-mon, and to call peaceably unto them. And Benjamin came again at that time; and they gave them wives which they had saved alive of the women of Ja'-besh-gil'-e-ad; and yet so they sufficed them. And the people repented them for Benjamin, because that the Lord had made a breach in the tribes of Israel.

Then the elders of the congregation said, How shall we do for wives for them that remain seeing the women are destroyed out of Benjamin? And they said, There must be an inheritance for them that be escaped of Benjamin, that a tribe be not destroyed out of Israel. Howbeit we may not give them wives of our daughters: for the children of Israel have sworn saying, Cursed be he that giveth a wife to Benjamin. Then they said, Behold, there is a feast of the Lord in Shil'-loh yearly in a place which is on the north side of Beth'-el, on the east side of the highway that goeth up from Beth'-el to She'-chem, and on the south of Le-bo'-nah. Therefore they commanded the children of Benjamin, saying, Go and lie in wait in the vineyards; And see, and, behold, if the daughters of Shi'-loh come out to dance in dances, then come ye out of the vineyards, and catch you every man his wife of daughters of Shi'-loh, and go to the land of Benjamin. And it shall be, when their fathers of their brethren come unto us to complain, that we will say unto them, Be favorable unto then for our sakes: because we reserved not to each man his wife in the war: for ye did not give unto them at this time, that ye should be guilty. And the children of Benjamin did so, and took them wives, according to their number, of them that danced, whom they caught: and they went and returned unto their inheritance, and repaired the cities, and dwelt in them. And the children of Israel departed thence at that time, every man to his tribe and to his family, and they went out from thence every man to his inheritance. In those days there was no king in Israel: every man did that which was right in his own eyes. (Judges 19-21)

This is a very interesting series of events that definitely shows that the Apostle Luke drew from since being a bit of historian. We see here that the man and his family elected not to go into the place where his brethren was not but wanted to stay within the family which he thought was more of family values. This is interesting because when the man found his family or his brethren they treated him worse than an enemy. This gives us great revelation in knowing that within the adversary attack he uses things and people that are close to us to bring about a down fall forewhich God uses that same thing as a elevation point to bring about a purging or a pruning. This causes us to grow deeper into the measuring of faith security that pushes us to perform, as the Lord wants us to. In that we see that the man and his family was in server danger and caused the destruction of someone close to him. This triggered a purging in the house of Israel and a movement that should have drawn them near to the Almighty.

Ultimately our battles is to draw us nearer to the Lord and to stay in that realm but we see by the end of this trial the people went back to doing the thing which was pleasing to their own eyes. But in the midst of the trial we see that Reuben answered the call of the people and joined the fight to move this people of godliness from Benjamin. It is unclear why Benjamin joins this fight against Israel. Maybe it could have been that it was their territory and they felt that because it was their territory they had to defend it. Out man and overwhelming odds Benjamin place a battle of epic proportion defending off Israel in two separate attacks. Israel went against Benjamin twice where they asked the Lord for counsel and was defeated. But this should be an eye opening for us to see that we have to stick and stay regardless of how the fight is looking and we have given our best shots. God knows the outcome to the battle and if we just obey and move within the guidance of God then we will see the victory. It is not in our time but in God's time.

God sent them out one more time that brought upon a plan that was to defeat the adversary spiritually before they could destroy it physically. When the Benjamites had placed good fight and it seemed that they would defeat them for the third time they knew not the evil coming against them. In that the attack plan forewhich was orchestrated by Israel was to place men in waiting and after they draw the Benjamites away from the city then sneak in and destroy the city by placing it up in flames, which crush the spirit of the Benjamites causing them to flee and ultimately be destroyed. But God's plan still in effect did not want the tribe totally wipe out. But wanted to remove the cancerous cell of the ungodliness within Benjamin and rehash the Benjamites with a new outlook. And the plan of God unfolded with one place was not in the congregation, which was in the land or territory of the half tribe of Manasseh. Took their virgins and give them to remaining six hundred to breed a resurrection of the Tribe of Benjamin.

This is what happens to us at times we have things and people in our lives that we want and God is trying to remove them from us and bring about a resurrection for a new thing in our lives. But we fight with God and finally the removal process brings about pain simply because it was the battle with the Lord that brought the pain about. We see here that the Tribe of Benjamin had a trait that could be dormant if it is not used properly and place not only in development but as well putting into action. The Tribe of Benjamin character grew into "compassion in action" which constantly needed purging to get the greatness out of the people. We will talk more about this in the section marked The Apostle Luke. But hold on to this in the building of the perfect character of Christ we see that first we must have the mindset which triggers a transformation of the heart that pushes something outwardly that is the very foundation of God Himself and evidence that we are of His kingdom. Now let us get into the next tribe so we can see if we can find the third transformation or third level in Christ as we move forward in our journey.

Simeon

Now let us look at the next tribe and person, which is Simeon and this, is a very interesting movement went on in his life as well as the tribe itself. Now before we get into this part I want you to understand that a lot of times it is not what is being said but what is not being said. Simeon tracing within the Bible is not as much as the rest of the tribes but it is very interesting in what they have. In this we have to look at every little thing to see the entire picture so that we can move into the framework of Simeon. We together is going to search the scriptures and look within the word of God and see what God have for us within Simeon. Let us get started.

Simeon simply means: "God hears" this has a very interactive meaning, which will reveal a lot to us as we go on within this particular book. Now Simeon was the second son of Jacob and Leah. Let us take a look at the birth of Simeon the Bible says: And when the Lord saw that Leah was hated, he opened her womb: but Ra'-chel was barren. And Leah conceived, and bare a son, and she called his name Reuben: for she said, Surely the Lord hath looked upon my affliction; now therefore my husband will love me. And she conceived again, and bare a son; and said, Because the Lord hath heard that I was hated, he hath therefore given me this son also: and she called his name Simeon. (Genesis 29:31-33) Now we know that Simeon was born at a time in Leah life where she was fighting for the love of Jacob and a constant rivalry between her and Rachel. Leah considered that God hand heard her in the time of need and given her a son that would have to draw her husband to her and give her the love that she was looking for.

Interesting how we can take what God has given us and tries to fit it in our lives as this or that and miss the true essence of the precious gifts of God. You see in this birth Simeon was place in the middle simply because the Bible indicates that Leah bore three sons consecutively as if Leah was giving birth between a period of two years to two in a half years three sons. In this is the key to the growing of the boys within a house with great tension and great stress upon the ladies within the camp. Leah giving birth first and giving birth to three sons, which the Bible let us know that Jacob loved Rachel more than he loved Leah. This is very interesting to see the magnitude of the house would be elevated. Now within the ladies were as if a competition for the love of Jacob but Jacob heart was set upon Rachel. But the Bible is very specific in how Jacob viewed each woman. Rachel was beautiful and Leah had tender eyes. This might explain the since of Jacob heart simply because it was not based upon the woman character but simply placed in a lustful setting that place the women in combat.

If this is true then we know that each woman know their standard for the time that they entered into the marriage to Jacob. Leah knew that she was one that was sort of tricked unto Jacob bed and Leah was wanted in the bed. This seems to give the idea that one woman was accepted and the other woman was wanted. Now in that gave one woman as we can say an edge upon another simply because the women knew that the situation that is here is not because of their doing but their father's Laban that attached both sisters together. Simply put the situation was ultimately in the hands of God forewhich neither woman had know help in placing them in this position but have the recoil of the situation. So within the plan of God we see and very important revelation that bears great impact upon our existence within the physical plain to supercede spiritually. God places us with areas that we have known hand in the situation and we are receiving the backlash or the recoil of the situation. In this we see that every situation is not a direct link to us but have a direct influence on us to create the character that is needed to move forward in the Body of Christ. You see here in this situation Leah had to learn to deal with the fact of the law of the land and her people to be wed to a man that did not love her as much as she wanted. But loved her sister more and this is a taxing situation from the beginning for you and I. We cannot comprehend sisters marring the same man because of the times that we live in but we have to look at it from the time frame forewhich they lived in. And we have to get away from that mindset of what I would have done if I were back there and peer into the word of God with the mindset of the characters that is given unto us here. This is were we will find the message from God to us and this will reveal the principle forewhich you and I can implement in our lives to achieve the level of learning forewhich God has for us here.

You see in this is the principle that took place from the very beginning of the birth of Simeon that was passed along to the Tribe of Simeon. We see that the women had to learn the acceptance of the situation and learn to understand what God has for them within the situation that will elevate them to the position within the Body of Christ that God wanted them to be. You see that is the same thing that God is calling from you and me today. If we stop focusing on the mess and look toward the heavens and try to set ourselves in position to hear the Lord as He is speaking to us in the situation or circumstance then and only then can we truly understand why God place us in this situation or circumstance and move toward an effective outcome. Remember God never puts to much on us than we can bear and always provide a door out we have to understand that some times God raises the standards up against the situation and we choose the standard that fits this area and apply it to the situation and the door appears.

Now this is very interesting simply because we have to remember that each tribe was place under the standard of one tribe. In that one standard was three separate characters that combined in the fullness presents one of the traits of Jesus Christ himself which gives us the formula forewhich you and I need to keep up front in our journey. You see as we move along in our Christian walk we grow and there is an order to everything that God does and in that order is a revealing as we can understand. In the understanding is the revelation to the truth of God that releases the principle of God that we can implement into our lives that propels us and many different areas of our lives. Now we also have to understand that in the standards that are lifted the trait that is used to move one from a situation into a blessing have to be applied. We see here that two women placed in a situation forewhich they had no say so over. But within the situation there is some growing that is needed to fulfill the position forewhich God needs for them to be in. This position is not just leaning on them but as well as the children because the mother is the first teacher of the child. If the mother is not where she suppose to be then the children don't get what they need and they have to start off in away to correct what was implanted as fact. In that places the child in a receiving position from the parents the things that they should not do but they see the parents or parent do it and they figure it have to be right.

But some situations forewhich the parents get into they have know influence on how they got there but it is in their power to grow within the situation. Grow spiritually that triggers a physical blessing that gives evidence to the fact that you are growing spiritually. In these two women they needed to grow simply because in the beginning there was no children but now the women see that there are children in the midst. The question is did the children pick up on the tension and the competition between the women? As well what was the children picking up from those private conversation between mother and son? What would you tell a child in that position about the other woman or the situation period? Remember at that time period that the children stayed with the mother until they have been weaned off from the mother. In this they spent a great deal of their early development with the mother and the father would come in from work or the synagogue and spend a little time with the child.

Now Jacob have three sons from a woman he did not love as much as he loved Rachel and the Bible refers to that Leah was hated. In that hate God was move by grace to intercede and bring forth fruit that causes a transformation of one thing into another. In Jacob's case how did he deal with the women conflict? Did he just over look it because it was customary for the women in the household to be against one another? Did his father teach him how to deal with more than one wife at a time along with the society that he was living in gave a helping hand in the development of his thinking in this type of situation? I believe in the society forewhich they lived in and his father gave him a training of how to deal with two separate women in the camp. Let us not forget that Jacob's grandfather had a problem with women in the same camp that was probably a great influence upon Jacob. In order to get the fullness of this we will have to look at this.

God had come to Abraham and told him that he would have a son that was be the receiver of the promise of all that God had promise him. But Abraham was old and his wife and they come up together with a plan that was suppose to be helping God but instead setting the stage for a war that last until this day. The Bible says: Now Sa'-rai Abram's wife bare him no children: and she had an handmaid, an Egyptian whose name was Ha'-gar. And Sa'-rai said unto A-bram, Behold now, the Lord hath restrained me from bearing: I pray thee, go in unto my maid; it may be that I may obtain children by her. And Abram hearkened to the voice of Sa'-rai Abram's wife took Ha'-gar her maid the Egyptian, after Abram had dwelt ten years in the land of Canaan, and gave her to her husband Abram to be his wife. And he went in unto Ha'-gar, and she conceived: and when she saw that she had conceived, her mistress was despised in her eyes. And Sa'-rai said unto Abram, My wrong be upon thee: I have given my maid unto thy bosom; and when she saw that she had conceived, I was despised in her eyes: the Lord judge between me and thee. But Abram said unto Sa'-rai, Behold, thy maid is in thy hand; do to her as it pleaseth thee. And when Sa'-rai dealt hardly with her, she fled from her face. And the angel of the Lord found her by a fountain of water in the wilderness, by the fountain in the way to Shur. And he said Ha'-gar, Sa-rai's maid, whence camest thou? and whither wilt thou go? And she said, I flee from the face of my mistress S'-rai. And the angel of the Lord said unto her, Return to thy mistress and submit thyself under her hands.

And the angel of the Lord said unto her, I will multiply thy seed exceedingly, that it shall not be numbered for multitude. And the angel of the Lord said unto her, Behold, thou art with child, and shalt bear a son, and shalt call his name Ish'-ma-el; because the Lord hath heard thy affliction. And he will be a wild man; his hand will be against him; and he shall dwell in the presence of all his brethren. And she called the name of the Lord that spake unto her, Thou God seest me: for she said, Have I also here looked after him that seeth me? Wherefore the will was called Be'-er-lahai'-roi; behold, it is between Ka'desh and Be'-red. And Ha'-gar bare Abram a son: and Abram called his son's name which Ha'-gar bare, Ish'-ma-el. And Abram was fourscore and six years old, when Ha'-gar bare Ish'-ma-el to Abram. (Genesis 16: 1-16) So here we see that Jacob's grandfather had trouble with the women in the household and when the children was born even tensified the situation. Let us see how this unfolded.

Now the Lord visited Abram and changed his name to Abraham and Sarai to Sarah and Sarah bored a son in the old age of Abraham forewhich he called his name Isaac. The Bible says: And the Lord visited Sarah as he had said, and the Lord did unto Sarah as he had spoken. For Sarah conceived, and bare Abraham a son in his old age, at the set time o which God had spoken to him. And Abraham called the name of his son that was born unto him, whom Sarah bare to him, Isaac. And Abraham circumcised his son Isaac being eight days old, as God had commanded him. And Abraham was an hundred years old, when his son Isaac was born unto him. And Sarah said, God hath made me to laugh, so that all that hear will laugh with me. And she said, Who would have said unto Abraham, that Sarah should have given children suck? for I have born him a son in his old age. And the child grew, and was weaned: and Abraham made a great feast the same day that Isaac was weaned. And Sarah saw the son of Ha'-gar the Egyptian, which she had born unto Abraham, mocking.

Wherefore she said unto Abraham, Cast out this bondwoman and her son: for the son of this bondwoman shall not be heir with my son, even with

Isaac. And the thing was very grievous in Abraham's sight because of his son. And God said unto Abraham, Let it not be grievous in thy sight because of the lad, and because of they bondwoman; in all that Sarah hath said unto thee, hearken unto her voice; for in Isaac shall thy seed be called. And also of the son of the bondwoman will I make a nation, because he is thy seed. And Abraham rose up early in the morning, and took bread, and a bottle of water, and gave it unto Ha'-gar, putting it on her shoulder, and the child, and sent her away: and she departed, and wandered in the wilderness of Be'-er-she'-ba. And the water was spent in the bottle, and she cast the child under one of the shrubs. And she went, and sat her sown over against him a good way off, as it were a bowshot: for she said, Let me not see the death of the child. And she sat over against him, and lift up her voice, and wept. And God heard the voice of the lad; and the angel of God called to Ha'-gar out of heaven, and said unto her, What aileth thee, Ha'-gar? fear not; for God hath heard the voice of the lad where he is.

Arise, lift up the lad, and hold him in thine hand; for I will make him a great nation. And God opened her eyes, and she saw a well of water; and she went, and filled the bottle with water, and gave the lad drink. And God was with the lad; and he grew, and dwelt in the wilderness, and became an archer. And he dwelt in the wilderness of Pa-ran: and his mother took him a wife out of the land of Egypt. (Genesis 21: 1-21) We can see how the stage was set for the attack upon the household forewhich the handmaiden had no say so in the situation and was brought back to the mistress by obeying the Lord command and submit herself. This is interesting simply because we know that the children was close in age and most likely developed a bond between each other. Having the same father but different mothers brought froth great tension forewhich Abraham dealt with it through the intervention of the Lord. This is the key to situation which you had know had in making but the Lord place you in that situation to obtain something that will prepare one for the movement that is coming in their life.

But the question here is did this have any effect upon the children as they were separated not fully understanding at the time why but being pulled apart for the glorification unto the Lord. But let us not forget the entire situation that was at hand not only did he grow up in a household where the women were at conflict but the inheritance of Abraham was at hand as well. Interesting how releasing the child of the handmaiden brought forth that not only did Isaac receive the material blessing of the firstborn but as well had the spiritual blessing in caring the covenant between God and Abraham. So the younger was the receiver of the blessing of God instead of the older and the younger inheritance was as the firstborn. We see the same situation appears in Isaac life as well with his children, Jacob and Esau. In Jacob character makeup the traits where alive in the blessing or the firstborn as well as the spiritual blessing of God and the inheritance of the situations stemming from more than one woman in the household.

Forewhich we know comes from the grandfather and from the father certain situations and events that accord to them were as if passed down to the children by way of being taught or molded in the early stages of their lives that held deep within the character makeup of each individual. This gives us great revelation and insight to our own character makeup where we see that passing down of traits from which the dominant person in our lives left their mark upon us. In this we have to see that the movement of us out of order can be the direct link to our children being out of order by learning from the mistakes we made but not knowing how to deal with what they have saw as well as learned.

What was passed upon Simeon as he grew up within a home of stress and tension that most definitely had an impact upon the molding of his character? This is most important simply because to overcome what was in his past to what was going on in his life that day effects the outcome of tomorrow forewhich Simeon had to develop in. Now Simeon development was linked to others that had great influences upon him as if his connection was under constant attack forewhich if found the right position would be a force to be reckon with. But in the development of that particular thing in its infancy stage it was moved in many directions forewhich caused great destruction within the molding of others that surrounded him. Do you remember the event that took place between Levi and Simeon the second and third son born to Leah in the span of time that made them close by nature? Remember how they tricked the Hivites of Shechem and massacred all the males because one of them had raped Dinah, their sister.

Interesting within the situation that what we call now a catch twenty-two, on one hand they were compelled because of what happened to their sister and wanted something to be done about it. The coming together of all the brothers in agreement as if to flow a particular reasoning but as if the two brothers broke the pack, Simeon and Levi. One the priestly heritage, and the other the foundation heritage of God's house, and this is very interesting by nature itself. Sometimes in the walk of a Christian is faced with decisions that cause one to seek out the same mindset as Simeon. This makes one to seek out the same mind thought, to justify a reaction outside of the revelation of God principles to revenge ones hurt or pain. Then act upon the situation or thought and as if the action had to be done simply out of the illusion forewhich the adversary has placed there. Remember friends that the foundation must stay intact in order for the house to stay together, not mix one part of the foundation with this and then take this out of it on the other side of the foundation.

God's revelation is complete to ensure that we as His people come forth with the victory at all times; we just sometimes cannot see it with the naked eye so we have to use our spiritual eye because the physical see the devastation, but the spiritual see the glory of the Lord working. This is interesting because what makes a person spiritually blind. In Simeon case in this situation Simeon was probably about 10 years older than Dinah. Dinah was the sister to twelve brothers that most likely as all families was teased and grew close to her brethren as they felt they had to protect her. So it was probably the physical connection that blinded the spiritual eye of Simeon that moved him toward the destruction of the Hivites. We see how everything is connected and there is no luck or what ever you like to call it playing out in the will of God. In this we have to take in accordance everything that befalls upon us and look through the spiritual and see what God has indeed for you and I.

As Simeon growth continued the development of his character he most likely faced some situations and circumstances that further moved him in loosing the false illusion forewhich the adversary was using him and begin to grow in wisdom. You see it had to be that wisdom grew because of the destructive nature of the trait of anger in Simeon simply because of the molding of his trait anger would play a destructive role if not wisdom is applied. But what is so interesting that his father knew the same thing that was revealed about Simeon within the blessing of his father. The Bible says: Simeon and Levi are brethren; instruments of cruelty are in their habitations. O my soul, come not thou into their secret; unto their assembly, mine honour, be not thou united: for in their anger they slew a man, and in their selfwill they digged down a wall. Cursed be their anger, for it was fierce; and their wrath, for it was cruel: I will divide them in Jacob, scatter them in Israel. (Genesis 49:5-7) We see in the blessing of Jacob we see that the memory of their action with Levi is the turning point of their character building, which is interesting for you and I.

You see their key is the attachment with another that can pull them off the path simply because another can ignite them into a place forewhich a trait becomes so strong that it overwhelms their own ability to control. We see that in the anger of Simeon there is no bounds forewhich his anger will take them. In this wisdom had to be applied on that forewhich the standard had to be lifted. This is interesting simply because they were numbered with the standard of Reuben being there. Now we see that the Apostle Luke gives the fullness of the side of tabernacle that represented this stage of development of perfection within Jesus Christ as He walked this earth. Now the Apostle Luke looks deeply through his own historian background and God used that to move the Apostle Luke to pen such writings. Now in that we cannot get into it right now but the Apostle Luke wrote about the Man Christ which we will get to in the section marked Apostle Luke. Reuben ensign is "The Rising Sun" forewhich Simeon symbol is Dagger and Pitcher.

Now the symbols have a unique revelation but if we start diving into that we will have a whole book on our hands that will take us away from this book. So I will give just a summary their symbols relate to the pacific nature of the people as well as the connection between them and God within the given gifts as well as the spiritual growth within the character of them. Just the same as the stone itself gives evidence of their characters. We will address that and much more in the section marked The Tribe of Simeon. Let us continue with another situation that showed growth within the character of Simeon that is a little different. Within his journey Simeon found his anger aroused again and this time it was directed at his brethren Joseph. Along with his brothers they rose up against Joseph and sold him off into Egypt where he went through his trials and tribulations. But in this situation I want to focus on the part of where they came to Joseph unknowing he was their brother and was seeking food. The land was in a famine and the children of Israel went to Egypt to find food.

At this time their brother unknowing to them he had rose to second in command forewhich fulfill the dream forewhich he had that raised his brothers to anger. Now when a trait is more dominant than the character it tends to appear more than a person wishes to do. I the case of Simeon the Bible do not speak of this but for me it is the thing that the Bible doesn't say that is important as well. Simeon most likely showed his bitterness outwardly toward Joseph simply because the anger within him had come upon him and overwhelmed him. In this I can see how Simeon maybe spoke harsh to Joseph as well as treated him with abuse and showing no compassion toward his brother that was coming from the anger that overwhelmed him. In this I can see why Joseph chose him to place him in custody at the time when the brethren came for food. Some might miss this but I want to point it out that Joseph did not chose him to pay back but chose the one that was attached by physical measures as well as the one that was so angry all the time that Joseph wanted to know for himself if his brother had grown.

Simply within the meeting with Joseph, Simeon spoke not a word that was recorded as well he spoke nothing that was recorded when he was placed in bondage right before the eyes of his brethren. This was most likely orchestrated by God as a measure of testing the faith of Simeon not in his brothers but in the fact that regardless of what happen I am still with you. Second it gave Joseph a chance to monitor his brother's reaction while in his custody as well as see the miraculous change within the ability to handle his anger. This was probably a joyous occasion for Joseph to see the maturity level within his brother and see him conduct himself in a discipline manner and do not get out of control. Look at this with me the Bible says: If ye be true men, let one of your brethren be bound in the house of your prison: go ye, carry corn for the famine of your houses: But bring your youngest brother unto me; so shall you words be verified, and ye shall not die, And they did so. And they said one to another, We are verily guilty concerning our brother, in that we saw the anguish of his soul, when he besought us, and we would not hear: therefore is this distress come upon us. And Reuben answered them, saying, Spake I not unto you, saying, Do not sin against the child: and ye would not hear? therefore, behold, also his blood is required. And they knew not that Joseph understood them; for he spake unto them by an interpreter. And he turned himself about from them, and wept; and returned to them again, and communed with them, and took from them Simeon, and bound him before their eyes. (Genesis 42:19-24)

Totally interesting that Simeon was chosen but what is even more interesting to me that it gives no clear evidence that any brother step forward and told the lord of the land which was Joseph take me and let my brothers go. It gives more weight to the idea that Joseph made the chose for them as they reminded themselves of the past situation concerning sealing their brother. Where they did not know that it was Joseph and he was able to understand what they were saying as well as understood the situation forewhich they were talking about. In that he learned that this thing of the past with their brother has haunted them since it happen and the deception has been so embedded in them that they cannot get rid of the guilt that is eating them alive. It moves Joseph so much that he wept and then took Simeon. Now they have to go home and tell their father, Jacob about what has happen as well as let him hear that one of his sons is in the hand's of the lord of the land. Let us take a look at this together.

And they came unto Jacob their father unto the land of Canaan, and told him all that befell unto them; saying, The man, who is the lord of the land, spake roughly to us, and took us or spies of the country. And we said unto him, We are true men; we are no spies: We be twelve brethren, sons of our father; one is not, and the youngest is this day with our father in the land of Canaan. And the man, the lord of the country, said unto us, Hereby shall I know that ye are true men; leave one of your brethren here with me, and take food for the famine of your households, and be gone: And bring your youngest brother unto me: then shall I know that ye are no spies, but that ye are true men: so will I deliver you your brother, and ye shall traffick in the land. And it came to pass as they emptied their sacks, that, behold, every man's bundle of money was in his sack: and when both they and their father saw the bundles of money, they were afraid. And Jacob their father said unto them, Me have ye bereaved of my children: Joseph is not, and Simeon is not, and ye will take Benjamin away: all these things are against me. And Reuben spake unto his father, saying, Slay my two sons, if I bring him not to thee: deliver him into my hand, and I will bring him to thee again. And he said, My son shall not go down with you: for his brother is dead, and he is let alone: if mischief befall him by the way in the which ye go, then shall ye bring down my gray hairs with sorrow to the grave. (Genesis 42: 29-38)

Now we see here the deep sorrowful pain that this news brought upon Jacob as well as how deep the news and action was to the brethren. In this situation we see that growth is tested and tested again to see if the security is base upon the foundation of truth and not trying to builded upon bad ground. We know the rest of the story that Simeon was return as well as Benjamin and the brothers found their brother and the father was released from his sorrow. In this is the shouting of Praise God for the security within the knowledge of Jesus Christ that is exploding here in this situation. We see in the developing of Simeon character the trait that was so explosive came under submission to the will of God and the growth was tested not for the failure in the test but the security of the anchor forewhich gives us an effective measure of faith that produces an effective product that will enhance the Body of Christ and glorify God.

You see Simeon had to develop within his character measures and means to bring under submission traits that where so overwhelming that it almost destroyed him. In this we learn that because we are unable to control a thing is not the reason not to control it but to come to the realization that it is only God that can help me with it and I need him. Within Simeon he had to learn the fact that he had to come to the understanding that he was going in a destructive path that has brought upon a transformation for what I was supposed to be to this monster that I do not even recognize. You most likely somewhere Simeon had to realize that a change is needed and he had to "Willingness" to make this possible in his life. You see you can want a many things but the key is to be willing to do what it takes to get what you want. Here is the key to that, that our willingness is the connection of submitting to the will of God and in that is the glorifying God and edifying the Body of Christ.

You see we have become willing to submit to the will of God and understand that everything is for the molding of my character and the security by faith in the word of God that God can and will on my behalf. In this we have the assurance of God place deep within that pulls forth "Willingness" and submission unto God word and brings about an embracing of the trials and tribulations that comes forth. Simply because we know that every situation and circumstance is a chance for you and I to edify the Body of Christ and glorify God in our movement within the situation or circumstance. Let us look at the continuation of the character of Simeon, as it is pass along within the Tribe of Simeon.

The Tribe of Simeon

Now we are going to move in to the Tribe of Simeon and see what the Lord has for us here. First a foremost we want to look at the prophecy of Simeon and understand that when Moses was blessing the nations Simeon was omitted which might be explain in the prophecy of Jacob. The Bible says: Simeon and Levi are brethren: instruments of cruelty are in their habitations. O my soul, come not thou into their secret: unto their assembly, mine honour, be not thou united: for in their selfwill they digged down a wall. Cursed be their anger, for it was fierce: and their wrath, for it was cruel: I will divide them in Jacob, and scatter them in Israel. (Genesis 49: 5-7) In this we can see the prophecy of Jacob coming true when Moses did not bless them simply because they were appear that the tribe of Simeon had been assimilated into the tribe of Judah, thus fulfilling Jacob's prophecy. Before we go even deeper into this let us start at the beginning so we can receive the fullness of this particular section.

Simeon had six sons: the Bible says: And the sons of Simeon; Jem'-u-el, and Ja'-min, and O'-had, and Ja'-chin and Zo'-har, and Sha'-ul the son of a Ca'-naan-i-tish woman: these are the families of Simeon. (Exodus 6:15) Now only five sons made up the Simeonites. The Bible says: The sons of Simeon after their families: of Nem'-u-el, the family of the Nem'-u-el-ites: of Ja'-min, the family of the Ja'-min-ites: of Ja'-chin, the family of the Ja'-chin-ites: Of Ze'-rah, the family of the Zar'-hites: of Sha'-ul the family of the Sha'-u-lites. These are the families of the Simeonites, twenty and two thousand and two hundred. (Numbers 26:12-13) The son that was not mention is O-had. Jemuel the oldest son of Simeon and his name mean: "God is light." Jamin means: "right hand; south." Jachin name means: "God will establish." Zerah name means: "spout" and Shaul name means: "asked of God." I wanted the meaning of the names present to just show you something. Let us put them together: God is light, right hand: south, God will establish, spout, asked of God. This is interesting watch this: God is light and His right hand God will establish a spout ready for all that is asked of God.

It is as if Simeon was making a statement with his children unto the world as well as the Body of Christ, which reveals a great revelation. In the wording and the direction it is going it gives the appearance that Simeon growth of willingness unlock a door for him that when he entered in it was the haven of rest which God had promised. The very first child gave evidence that in the willingness development something is released that secures one within the true awesomeness of God. God is light, knowledge, and enlightment or free from ignorance, prejudice, etc. so we can say God is knowledge and free from ignorance, prejudice, etc. or enlightment. So how about we break down the entire statement and see what is revealed right before us. God is knowledge and enlightment and with the right hand

and the southside God will establish or ordain a spout of living water for our things asked of God. This is very powerful simply because with the very foundation of the southside of the tabernacle I will give my right hand Jesus Christ to become a spout of living waters that is ordain for our things asked of God. This brought a very interesting explosion within my spirit when I notice this and I wanted to share with you this marvelous revelation here. In growth the maturity level will reveal revelation unto you that is so profound that it goes even pass your own comprehension to comprehend. We see that this very essence of the foundation of the southside hold the truth to the firmness of the foundation that pushes forward before us to let others see that this must be God. I want you to be able to see how the Apostle Luke being a historian drew from what he knew and implemented the principles in his life that pushed out this foundation unto the world that brought forth a willing vessel to submit himself to pen two letters that has brought upon revelations and principles of God that can and will set us free.

The Apostle Luke being a historian could have found this in his learning process but realized that what they were looking for he had the presence of in his life. In this the Apostle Luke saw first hand the foundation of God working in performance of Jesus Christ as well as the father simply because it was Him that wanted to reconciled with His creation. Within the Tribe of Simeon we see that they numbered at one time 59,300 fighting men in the first census in the wilderness and 22,200 at the second. When the land of Canaan was divided the second lot fell to the Tribe of Simeon. They received land in the extreme southern part of Canaanites in the middle of Judah's territory. This gives us conformation that the tribe was being absorbed into the Tribe of Judah at this time. This is interesting in a since by understanding the character of Simeon and the traits forewhich help develop their character we see the necessity to be absorbed by one that the very essence of their true deliverance is the very foundation which is being taught here. You see Judah means to praise but the very essence of the foundation that is present in the southside of the tabernacle is the essential part of the catalyst for praise. This gives evidence that our praise is attach to something that is the very essence of Jesus Christ Himself that causes a reaction from the Heavenly Host to respond.

We see in the absorption that they went through their trials and tribulations. One was when Judah fought with Canaanites and Simeon united with them. The Bible says: Now after the death of Joshua it came to pass, that the children of Israel asked the Lord, saying, Who shall go up for us against the Ca'-naan-ites first, to fight against them? And the Lord said, Judah shall up: behold, I have delivered he land into his hand. And Judah said unto Simeon his brother, Come up with me into my lot, that we may fight against the Ca'-naan-ites; and I likewise will go with thee into thy lot. So Simeon went with him. And Judah went up; and the Lord delivered the

Ca'-naanites and the Per'-iz-zites into their hand: and they slew of them in Be'-zek ten thousand men. And they found A-don'-i-be'-zek in Be'-zek: and they fought against him, and they slew the Ca'-naan-ites and the Per'-iz-zites. But A-don-i-be'-zek fled; and they pursued after him, and caught him, and cut off his thumbs and his great toes. And A-don'-i-be'-zek said, Threescore and ten kings, having their thumbs and their great toes cut off, gathered their meat under my table: as I have done, so God hath requited me. And they brought him to Jerusalem, and there he died. Now the children of Judah had fought against Jerusalem, and had taken it, and smitten it with the edge of the sword, and set the city on fire. And afterward the children of Judah went down to fight against the Ca'-naan-ites, that dwelt in the mountain, and in the south, and in the valley.

And Judah went against the Ca'-naan-ites that dwelt in He'-bron: (now the name of He'-bron before was Kir'-jath-ar'-ba:) and they slew She'-shai, and A-hi'-man and Tal'-mai. And from thence he went against the inhabitants of De'-bir: and the name of De'-bir before was Kir'-jath-se'-pher: And Caleb said, He that smiteth Kir'-jath-se'-pher, and taketh it, to him will I give Ach'-sah my daughter to wife. And Oth'-ni-el the son of Ke'-naz, Caleb's younger brother, took it: and he gave him Arch'-sah his daughter to wife. And it came to pass, when she came to him that she moved and she lighted from off her ass; and Caleb said unto her, What wit thou? And she said unto him, Give me a blessing: for thou hast given me a south land; give me also springs of water. And Caleb gave her the upper springs and the nether springs. And the children of the Ken'-ite, Moses' father in law, went up out of the city of palm trees with the children of Judah into the wilderness of Judah, which lieth in the south of A'-rad; and they went and dwelt among the people.

And Judah went with Simeon his brother, and they slew the Ca'-naan-ites that inhabited Ze'-phath, and utterly destroyed it. And the name of the city was called Hor'-mah. Also Judah took Ga-za with the coast thereof, and Ads'-ke-lon with the coast thereof, and Ek'-ron with the coast thereof. And the Lord was with Judah; and he drave out the inhabitants of the mountain; but could not drive out the inhabitants of the valley, because they had chariots of iron. And they gave He'-bron unto Caleb, as Moses said: and he expelled thence the three sons of A'-nak. (Judges 1:1-20) Look at how the delivering power of God was in the hands of Simeon and Judah or better yet you can say it in these words "God hears praise" what a wonderful revelation. Together they became a force that the adversary had no defense for and the movement of God broke through and are molding the plan to unfold before you and I. Along with the territory of Simeon there was some great land that was given unto them, Beersheba, Hormah and Ziklag. These cities are lands forewhich had connections to the past of Israel as well as to the future of Israel.

As the tribe moved forward and continue in their calling and was absorbed by the Tribe of Judah they were not forgotten. The Bible says: And by the border of Benjamin, from the east side unto the west side, Simeon shall have a portion. And by the border of Simeon, from the east side unto the west side, Is'-sa-char a portion. (Ezekiel 48: 24-25) Look at how Ezekiel speaks of the gates and their position: The Bible says: And at the south side four thousand and five hundred measures: and three gates; one gate of Simeon, one gate of Is'-sa-char, one gate of Zeb-u-lun. (Ezekiel 48:33) The foundation is never forgotten and always present even as it is being absorbed within the different areas still it holds it own presence. In the book of Revelation Simeon is still numbered within the 144,000.

In our review we see that the character of Simeon is "Willingness" which has no boundaries if the fundamental grounding is based upon the richness of the truth in Christ Jesus. We saw within the developing of the trait that the connection within other areas still does not eliminate the presence of the character willingness. One thing we have to come to agreement with that our willingness is the door used by God to propel us in the direction forewhich God molds us to what we need to be to fulfill His will for our lives. In this we see that the process is not instant and takes work simply because we maintain a building process upon the wisdom or kingship mentality. This brings about the transformation of the heart that pushes the elements that compounded together create an action that totally places the pure essence of God. We see this within the character of The Apostle Luke with his historian background caught hold to the true essence of Christ through the foundation that moved him. Remember, "God is knowledge and enlightment and with the right hand and the southside God will establish or ordain a spout of living water for our things asked of God."

Forewhich they were looking for we have and in that we are awaiting His return for the glorification of God. We have been empowered by God to call things out of the atmosphere to attach itself to the principle of God, which we implement in our lives. That starts a resurrection of our knew selves that causes us to represent God with the very foundation that brought about our spiritual resurrection. As we move on to the next tribe we will be building a foundation that produces an effective product that edifies the Body of Christ and glorify God. In this we will find a formula that will be revealed in the section marked The Apostle Luke that will explode within our spirits and release a great magnitude of revelation for you and I. We have to understand that the foundation is not the same foundation physically as it is represented spiritually. Let me explain a physical foundation is what is used to build upon but in spiritual foundation is the anchor for the process of building any thing. You see in the spiritual realm everything is build upon the foundation so that gives the foundation a spiritually moving part that sets the ground for building.

We constantly draw from the foundation within everything and every area forewhich we build upon in the Body of Christ. This is the same foundation forewhich was Jesus and at the same times the reason for Jesus Christ. We as members of the Body of Christ have to develop the character or trait of willingness in order to receive the transformation of what is being pushed out of the heart to be shown as a banner for those to see I am of Christ. Before we get ahead of ourselves let us go on to the next section.

Gad

Now we come to the final tribe on the southside forewhich does not mean it is the least. This particular tribe holds the thread that stitches everything together that once fully integrated in to the spiritual fabric then we see exactly what is made as this tribe pulls everything together. But in order to see the full magnitude of the tribe we need to understand the founder's character and see how his development affected the growing process of the tribe. In this I want you to see how the delicate spiritual material is woven together as if one is using gold for thread. In this we will reveal one of the most preached about things in the Bible but not fully understood until you are able to recognize it. You see having something and don't know how to use it is just as bad as looking for something and you don't know what it is. In Gad we will see the developing of a character forewhich you and I need to pay close attention to. This particular character is the back breaker of the adversary attacks as well as the most used tool in the arsenal of the Body of Christ. In that we will together see the make up of this particular trait and how the adversary targets it as well as the over coming with this particular character. I want you to remember that each character of the tribes mention here is traits that are lying dormant within some of the members in the Body of Christ.

You see we possess all the traits of our ancestors but what happens is that one trait becomes more dominant within us that are the tool used to develop our character. In that situations and circumstances becomes the spring boards of our emotional and psychological make up that feeds off of our primary trait that develops the character forewhich we present to others. What happens is that the adversary knows if the character is develop in the manner forewhich it was attended to be then it would become a force to strong for the adversary to deal with. Here is the key we know that the adversary is going to be on the job 24/7 attacking constantly trying to move us from the path that God has design for us but in that is the down fall of the adversary. You see with the constant attack each attack can be propelled before the adversary can even launch the attack. Once a person realize that the movement is orchestrated by God and is being used for the edifying of the members of the Body of Christ then we have an inside look at the adversary. Once we see within the attack it does not become an attack it becomes a blessing to see the molding process take place for our next elevation in Christ. In this we are not looking for the material gain but we are searching for the next level in Christ. This will bring about us seeking the kingdom of God first and all what our hearts desire will be added unto us. But we don't go into the arms of God looking for material gain we go as a vessel unshaped and need molding to be able to handle to the next elevation. You see if God gave you all that He has for you with out preparing you for what He is giving you then it would become a downfall for you and I because we could not handle the things properly.

You see with out removing the waste of the adversary penetration then we are burden with the attacks that are so embedded that it would drive us insane trying to defend off the attacks. But if we embrace the process of the molding through situations and circumstances and events in our lives then we can see the movement of God in our lives and our hearts would be filled with joy. You see everything in God is tested to be sure that the foundation of faith is secure in the word of God. So we are the vehicles used to spread the faith through our trials and tribulations that brings upon us an embracing of the process. This gives us power to stand before the adversary and know within our hearts that this is for our benefit and our molding and this is going to elevate me within the spiritual plain in faith so that I am secure in the word of God. Remember that if we stay in the word we are his disciples and we will know the truth and the truth will set us free from the bondage of the adversary attacks to see them for truly what they are. In seeing the attacks for what they truly are gives us confidence in knowing that the outcome is our benefit and the adversary can not form a weapon physically or spiritually that will have victory over me. Simply because I am in the hands of Christ and in that is the revelation that know one can pluck me out of his hands and giving up my body is a sacrifice I do willingly to glorify the Father.

You see sacrifice of our body does not mean we are going to be hanging from the cross that was Christ position for us but our part is the resurrection in Christ that gives us freedom against the adversary. So let us prepare ourselves to receive what God has for us in Gad. Remember this as we go along that the word of God is not just a gathering of stories and the writings of a few telling of the past and the future. The Bible is alive and is interwoven together that holds the keys to spiritual maturity and give ammunition to the receiver of the revelation the ability to be set free. In this we are being conform and transform into the image of Christ Jesus to become an effective product that will produce an awesome deliverance to all those that come in contact with you as well as one that will shake the very foundation of Hell itself. This is the goal that we as members in the Body of Christ to become so Christ like that the adversary means and method of attack seems to be as soft cotton falling upon us. As well as a beacon of light that shines like the son that sends off signals to those that are lost and draw those out from the land of darkness. But in order to achieve such a level in Christ Jesus we have to take the foundation and stand on it and move on it and speak it and show it to the entire world and this will transcend one into the realm forewhich everything is seen from the spirit.

You see we constantly say that the Bible fits together but what is so strange that the average members in the Body of Christ do not know how it fits together or how the word of God works. We need to constantly be looking for a deeper revelation in God's word to edify the Body of Christ and glorify God in this we see how the word of God is connected. The connection is in three areas, physical, psychological, and spiritual. In those area are woven fabric that is empowered by the thread spun together that makes these areas stronger, better, to be used by God as a willing vessel. Within the Gad and the Tribe of Gad is the thread that will pull the word of God together and let us see how the intertwining is secure in the word of God and the needle is implementing the principles in our lives. Now let us see this in Gad right now.

Now Gad was the seventh of Jacob twelve sons and the firstborn of Zilpah. In this situation is great revelation that illuminates the pure essence of the woven thread through out the word of God. The Bible says: And when Ra'-chel saw that she bare Jacob no children, Ra'-chel envied her sister; and said unto Jacob, Give me children, or else I die. And Jacob's anger was kindled against Ra'-chel: and he said, Am I in God's stead, who hath withheld from thee the fruit of the womb? And she said, Behold my maid Bil'-hah, go in unto her; and she shall bear upon my knees, that I may also have children by her. And she gave him Bil'-hah her handmaid to wife: and Jacob went in unto her. And Bil'-hah conceived, and bare Jacob a son. And Ra'-chel said, God hath judged me, and hath given me a son: therefore called she his name Dan. And Bil'-hah Ra'-chel's maid conceived again, and bare Jacob a second son. And Ra'-chel said, With great wrestling have I wrestled with my sister, and I have prevailed: and she called his name Naph'-ta-li.

When Leah saw that she had left bearing she took Zil'-pah her maid, and gave her Jacob to wife. And Zil'-pah Leah's maid bare Jacob a son. And Leah said, A troop cometh: and she called his name Gad. (Genesis 30: 1-12) Interesting how both women place were based upon the productivity of bearing children forewhich gave them security within themselves of being who they suppose to be. In other words the women did not feel like a wife to her husband unless she was giving birth to a child. In this at that time in history the women felt that the more children they had the stronger the love between the man and the woman. As well it gave her sort of a status among the community to bare children for her husband especially a son. In this the women put their efforts toward to conquer the love of Jacob. At that time in the land it was legal for a wife to give her handmaiden to her husband for the bearing of children.

What happens is that the women give her handmaiden to the husband and he brings forth a child within her. The handmaidens have no rights of their own as if they are slaves to the mistress and must perform the duties given to her by her mistress. This was the custom and the law within the land, and then the handmaiden would deliver the child sitting upon the lap of the mistress. The mistress position themselves so that when the child comes forth it pass from the womb of the handmaiden pass the womb of the mistress which sets the stage of the deliverance through the womb of the mistress. This brings forth that the child is now of the handmaiden but the property of the mistress. This is the procedure forewhich Rachel was given her handmaiden over to Jacob for this particular reason.

Now in such a household Leah could see what was going on and probably knew the anger that was kindled against Rachel as she argued with Jacob about the child. But Leah felt that her worth was lessen at the time of the bearing of the child by Rachel handmaiden Bilhah. It is as if Leah gave herself a worth check and found since she was not bearing any more children and Jacob was spending time with her then he would lose his entrance in her. It weighed so heavy upon Leah till she come forth to Jacob and offered her handmaiden Zilpah to her husband. Now watch this both women was focus so much upon their worth to the man that they removed God completely out of the situation and even with one woman was tending to blame God for her not having children. In this the adversary had penetrated them by way of customs and belief that brought both women to a point of offering another to fulfill their desires that was legal in the land. Here we know that what the adversary thought was destruction was the continuing of the unfolding revelation of God to fulfill the will of God in the two handmaidens.

Now the question is that would the will of God would have been fulfilled if the two women had not done what they did. The question is simple and the answer is yes God will have been fulfill one way or another. But the pain of the situation would have been avoided if their eyes were set upon the kingdom of God instead of the traditional outlook upon themselves if they did not bear children. It is the same for you and I if we do not have certain things or not in the right group that society view us as nothing. We struggle for attention as well as love from each other as if it is what we need in order to be what we need to be and forgetting that it is the heavens that make us who we are and all that we need to get where we are intended to be. We give up all that we are and all that we have in order to get what we want from another if it is his or her love to just being in their company to satisfy an urge that is so deep that it blinds us from all other things and paths. We get to a point that desperation is leaping from within us as light from a light bulb and everyone sees it and nobody says a word. It is interesting when we are going on the right path people have something to say to take us off the path but when we are going through difficult things it seems that you are all alone and no one says a thing.

In the birth of Gad this same thing was at work were Leah judge herself worth and was isolated and had nothing to feed upon but her thoughts of worthlessness and reacted upon that feeling. She called a troop is coming and name him Gad forewhich it means "good fortune." What is interesting in this situation is that Leah said a "troop cometh" as if she was seeing something that no one else could see. What is the significant of a "troop cometh?" As if a flock or a group had come forth that was so massive and so great that she was being gathered in the number that came forth. The secret is in the meaning of the name "good fortune" that gives us the evidence of what was going on in the mind of Leah at that time. She receive a revelation that peeked within her spirit that brought her back to the realism that the kingdom of God is first and in that all that you desire will be given unto you. God's good fortune would be given unto them that seek him first in all things and by placing things in the hand of God then and only then can one have freedom from the attacks of the adversary.

You see the abundance of God's good fortune is a magnitude of abundance that cannot be measured simply because of the depths of mercy that God shows us. This particular tribe has the sweetest traits that combined to bring forth our walk as Christians that produces light and life to the world. I want you to understand that yes this is the only tribe that has a two-fold character that responds together to bring about the character forewhich the Lord Christ Jesus characteristics of a Man is fulfilled in us. As if our humanity is preserved in this character, as if the Apostle Luke was inspired to focus deep within this as he wrote the words that in the Gospel of Luke and the Book of Acts blossoms with deep revelation for you and I. This revelation will give the Body of Christ Jesus the principle of the very essence of understanding the revelation of receiving the fullness of the spirit. Remember readers that God's blue print for you and I is the Holy Bible and in that blue print the very ability for you and I to receive God's revelation these traits must be in full swing within the body, mind, and soul. Without it we can never achieve anything within our quest to become exactly what God wants us to be, so let us together begin our walk together in search of the character that carry us to the next trial and gives us total victory in all areas.

Gad growing up years is not too much recorded in the word of God but as an individual it is not much recorded but as the tribe there is a lot more that was recorded. We know that Gad was present in the selling of Joseph but there is nothing recorded that Gad said in the situation, which is very interesting. Gad was the seventh son and at that time Joseph was most likely in his teenage years so that would most likely make him in his twenties, which is very interesting. Gad having nothing recorded simply suggest to you and I that his struggle in the situation was within and not outwardly. In this is a revealing of the fighting ground forewhich the adversary was using within this particular situation. It seems as if Gad moving with his brothers was attached to them through the means of following them without question regardless of what the situation or circumstance was. As if Gad might have felt that he was not strong enough to stop what was going to happen to Joseph and fear gripped him to the point that it choke him up.

Regardless of what the situation was with Gad at that time but we do no that it was not recorded that he said a word to prevent what was happening. In this we see that the development of his character was not based upon the situation but the reaction in him toward the situation. You see we can be molded by what we do as well as what we don't do. In this the revelation that everything has an effect upon us one way or another that gives either one or two things. One we can show the power of the Lord or the adversary uses the situation to penetrate our spiritual grid to weaken us. We see in this situation the adversary used it to penetrate Gad's spiritual grid to cause destruction but it seems that Gad rose up to the battle within and moved forward in the developing his character. Interesting how he grew where we fine how Moses praised Gad for his bravery and faithfulness to duty. Let us take a look at this so we can receive the full magnitude of the situation or circumstance to see what God is revealing to us. The Bible says: And of Gad he said, Blessed be he that enlargeth Gad: he dwelleth as a lion, and teareth the arm with the crown of the head. And he provided the first part for himself, because there, in a portion of the lawgiver, was he seated; and he came with the heads of the people, he executed the justice of the Lord, and his judgments with Israel. (Deuteronomy 33:20-21)

This is very interesting because of the prophecy of Jacob about Gad. Let take a look at the blessing of Jacob: the Bible says: Gad a troop shall overcome him: but he shall overcome at the last. (Genesis 49:19) We see here that in the beginning the development of the character would fall short of the attacks of the adversary simply because of the lack of understanding of what is going on and who they are. The overwhelming of the situations and circumstances will overcome him in a sense that he is spiritually weak do to the development process not fully matured. Which this releases in our spirit simply because we have not reached the ability to fight off today does not mean that I will not become stronger, better, and grow in maturity that the same attack will not have the same effect. This is wonderful to know simply because if it seems that we are defeated we see that within the prophecy of Jacob or the blessing of Jacob that Gad might have been weak in the beginning but he will mature and grow in strength over a period of time. In that we have to see the embracing of the situation that gives us evidence of the area forewhich we need to work on or strengthen so that we can become effective product that the adversary is repelled. This is the key that because I am weak today does not mean I will not grow stronger from the attack but it gives evidence that the Lord has strength for me once I start to implement the will of God in our lives. Let us continue with Gad.

You see the key here is to be totally emerged in the will and the plan of God that we strip away all the fleshly desires and search for only what God wants for us. Let me ask you readers, have this every happen to you that you wanted something so bad that you did not even care if it was in the plan or will of God for you to have it. You went after this person or thing until you got your hands on it and once you got it you found out that it was not what you really wanted. What is so interesting about that, we will convince ourselves that this was exactly what I wanted. But everyone around you sees that this thing or person is not good for you. Before you admit that it is not any good for you it would take the heavens to open before you and God Almighty just tap you on the head. Do you remember what got you that far are the same things that must take you away or out of the situation? This enlightens us with deep revelation about the traits that is needed to enhance our walk with the Lord. Interesting how most traits has the ability to be used incorrectly and causes havoc in our life.

In order to stay in the place forewhich we receive not only the fullness of the spirit as well as the gift that magnifies the presence of the Lord in our life. In order to do that the traits and characters is booming in the situation that caused the birth of Gad. Remember Christians that we are a work in progress that don't mean that we stand in line for our process. What it means is that with the characteristics of the qualities of traits that develop our character needs to be constantly worked on by our own ability by the power of God's intervention. Other words through God's help you and I can come closer together with the true revelation of the word of God exploding in our spirits and these traits are in the heart of the explosion. You see regardless of what is going on there is something that can repel the adversary and move you through a situation and circumstance that others think you should have not made it through.

You see Gad possess a character that holds the key to victory as well as the thread that pulls everything together and brings about a strong and powerful spiritual grid. This simply happens when we make ourselves willing as we grow in compassion and place this into action that is revolved around one thing that gives the power source to the movement forewhich God has called us to do. You see Gad character is "Dedication and Determination" which is two powerful forces combine that breaks yolks and bondages of the adversary. We have to be dedicated to the Lord regardless of what is going on in our lives as well as how the flesh rear its ugly head we must stay dedicated to the Lord. The word "Dedicated" means: "devoted" and devoted means: very loving, loyal, or faithful. In this we see the secret or the key to breaking the strongholds forewhich the adversary tries to destroy us. We find our victory in the faithfulness of our ability to stand on the word of God and be true or loyal to God that gives birth to the very essence of God, which is his love. In this we see the formula to break bondage in our lives, which is stay loyal or faithful to God Almighty and your break through is coming.

Now the "Determination" means: "firmness of purpose" which is a very interesting definition. Let us break this down to grasps the full meaning "firmness of purpose" simply means "solid possessing aim." I want you to understand that within the will of God we are given a solid foundation a rock to build upon every area of our lives constantly remembering that our destiny is to constantly keeping the kingdom of God first. In this we build a defense against the adversary as well as keep our course that will edify the Body of Christ as well as glorify God. You see Gad from the very beginning was recognize as a force "a troop coming" forewhich dedication and determination became the spring board of his character that carried him through to maturity in the Word of God. Interesting enough that the very character of Gad would become our bases of thread that pulls the entire word of God into the rightful position in our lives. In our Christian walk we have to remember that it is a solid foundation possessing aim toward the heavens that places us within the furnace to be molded and the same thing that brings us out of the furnace. Our situations and circumstances is the furnace forewhich God uses to mold us but if we stay determine and dedicated to the Lord then our molding will become our elevation in a great gift of God.

The Apostle Luke being a historian and a doctor understood that dedication and determination is the key to very essence of God wrapped up within the movement of God. We see that "compassion in action" and "willingness" and "determination and dedication" works hand in hand to unfold one of the greatest gifts forewhich the Lord had given unto man. This thing that drove the Apostle Luke to be used by God to pen two letters to a friend is the same thing that protects his path through a solid foundation and keeping his eye on the Lord. In this is the formula for breaking the strongholds forewhich the adversary has upon us. If we see the true essence of the attacks as the molding furnace forewhich the Lord uses to elevate us within the spirit. Then we see that if we move out in the very essence of Jesus Christ "compassion in action and keep a willingness about ourselves to submit to the will of God and be determine and dedicated then know attack that the adversary comes up with can withstand the power that will be release forewhich the Apostle Luke possessed. This do not mean that trouble will flee but what it does mean that you can cause the adversary to flee with the oppression of the attack and take away the negative force from the attack. In that we release the true essence of the attack and gain exactly what the Lord have for us in the midst of the attack. So let us go forth and see how this was passed along to the descendants of Gad and how God molded it to his perfection to move within the will of God.

The Tribe of Gad

Now here we get a chance to explore in depths the movement of God within the Tribe of Gad to develop their character of "Dedication and Determination." In other word Gad had a character of seriousness toward the Lord and the will of God in his life that was being develop constantly. So let us get start. Now Gad was fruitful and was the father of seven sons forewhich all founded tribal families. The Bible says: The children of Gad after their families: of Ze'-phon, the family of the Ze'-phon-ites: of Hag'-gi, the family of the Hag'-gites: of Shu'-ni, the family of the Shu'-nites: Of Oz'-ni, the family of the Oz'-nites: of E'-ri, the family of the E'-rites: Of A'-rod, the family of the Ar'-o-dites: of A-re'-li, the family of the A-re'-lites. These are the families of the children of Gad according to those that were numbered of them, forty thousand and five hundred. (Numbers 26:15-18) Now let us look at the children. Zephon means: "expectation" and Haggi means: "born on a feast day." Ozni means: "my hearing" and Eri means: "watchful." And Arod means: "hunchbacked" and Areli means: "heroic."

Now the symbol of Gad is three tents. The largest of the three is in the foreground at the center and the other two are on either side in the background. In those days the tent was the dwelling place of the children of Israel, the sons of Jacob. They never would live in houses until they came into the promise land, but Gad never fully inherited the land. So that simply means that they wondered around most of their lives never really settling down long in one place. In fact we have used his name Gad to coin an expression that means, "to wander about in an idle or restless ways as in seeking amusement." The Prophet Jeremiah, when teaching Israel said, "Why gaddest thou about so much to change thy way?" (Jeremiah 2:36)

Can you see the representation of another event that happens that was the greatest thing that has ever happen for the world? That event was the Lord our Savior on the cross. This was very important for me because this gave me the severity of the situation not coming into maturity for these particular traits that combine in making a character for Gad possessed. The word "tent" comes from the Hebrew word "ohel (o-hel)" which means: a covering, a home, a tabernacle, and a tent. The Bible says: For we know that if our earthly house of this tabernacle were dissolved, we have a building of God, an house not made with hands, eternal in the heavens. For in this we groan, earnestly desiring to be clothed upon with our house which is from heaven: If so be that being clothed we shall not be found naked. For we that are in this tabernacle do groan, being burdened: not for that we would be unclothed, but clothed upon, that mortality might be swallowed up of life. (2Corinthians: 5:1-4) In that we learn that the tabernacle is a sort of a body that was made not by hands but eternal in the heavens. So understanding the revelation that Gad was looking for the Messiah to come and we are looking for the return of the Messiah. That each of us have to still hand on to what exactly got Gad through will most defiantly get us through till we see the second coming of the Lord. What a wonderful God showing us exactly what is needed in order to obtain the exact thing that our forefathers receive and placing a blueprint for us so we will not lose our way.

The prophetic word of Gad by Moses is a tremendous prophesy and it is packed full of wonderful and interesting meanings. But Jacob's prophesy saw into the later times of Gad and their overcoming. Also check out the Gadites mentioned in the Bible. Eliasaph in Numbers 1:14 which reads "Of Gad; Eliasaph the son of Deuel." God has added there to Eliasaph the son of Deuel was the head of the Tribe of Gad, Geuel was one of he 12 spies who were sent to Canaan. Numbers 13:15 reads: "Of the tribe of Gad, Geuel the son of Machi." Which Machi means: wounded, beaten: He was the father of Geuel the spy. One might wonder what would have happened if all the tribes had taken their possessions on the west side of the Jordan. They probably would have squeezed out the giants and the enemies of Israel. But because they were spread out so thinly, much of the land that God had promised them was not possessed until much later. Even at the time of David the Jebusites held stronghold of what is called Jerusalem today. David's men took it in B. C. 1048 (400 years later) the Bible says: "And the Philistines took the ark of God, and brought it from Ebenezer unto Ashdod. When the Philistines took the ark of God, they brought it into the house of Dagon, and set it by Dagon. And when they of Ashdod arose early on the morrow, behold, Dagon was fallen upon his face to the earth before the ark of the Lord. And they took Dagon, and set him in his place again. And when they arose early on the morrow morning, behold, Dagon was fallen upon his face to the ground before the ark of the Lord; and the head of Dagon and both the palms of his hands were cut off upon the threshold; only the stump of Dagon was left to him.

Therefore neither the priests of Dagon, nor any that come into Dagon's house, tread on the threshold of Dagon in Ashdod unto this day. But the hand of the Lord was heavy upon them of Ashdod, and he destroyed them, and smote them with emerods, even Ashdod and the coasts thereof. And when the men of Ashdod saw that it was so they said, The ark of the God of

Israel shall not abide with us: for his hand is sore upon us, and upon Dagon our god. They sent therefore and gathered all the lords of the Philistines unto them, and said, What shall we do with the ark of the God of Israel? And they answered, Let the ark of the God of Israel be carried about unto Gath. And they carried the ark of the God of Israel about thither. And it was so, that, after they had carried it about, the hand of the Lord was against the city with a very great destruction: and he smote the men of the city, both small and great, and they had emerods in their secret parts. (1Samuel 5:1-9)

Interesting enough that when one is dedicated as well as determine to please the Lord it sometimes will conflict with ones that believe what we are doing is against God. You see when we are dedicated and determine in our movements to acknowledge God in always we tend to lean toward things that are against the religious outlook upon things as well as religious doctrine that pushes us against the grains of the particular sect or denomination. This is very important to understand simply because it is sometimes that the Lord uses one to turn an entire organization or a nation around to the point of seeing instead of in religious boundaries and come out to the realm of the spirit where God is moving. Remember my friends that denominations and organizations is not a bad thing what is bad is trying to mold God in fitting into such a small box that you lose the elevation within the spirit because it does not fit in the denomination or organization. Let us look at this within the Tribe of Gad.

The Bible says: Then Joshua called the Reu'-ben-ites, and the Gad'-ites, and the half tribe of Ma-nas'-seh, And said unto them, Ye have kept all that Moses the servant of the Lord commanded you, and have obeyed my voice in all that it commanded you: Ye have not left your brethren these many days unto this day, but have kept the charge of the commandment of the Lord your God. And now the Lord your God hath given rest unto your brethren, as he promised them: therefore now return ye, and get you unto your tents, and unto the land of your possession, which Moses the servant of the Lord gave you on the other side Jordan. But take diligent heed to do the commandment and the law, which Moses the servant of the Lord charged you, to love the Lord your God, and to walk in all his ways, and to keep his commandments, and to cleave unto him, and to serve him with all your heart and with all your soul. So Joshua blessed them, and sent them away: and they went unto their tents. Now to the one half of the tribe of Ma-nas'-seh, Moses had given possession in Ba'-shan: but unto the other half thereof gave Joshua among their brethren on this side Jordan sent them away also unto their tents, then he blessed them.

And he spake unto them, saying, Return with much riches unto your tents, and with very much cattle, with silver, and with gold, and with brass, and with iron, and with very much raiment: divide the spoil of your enemies with your brethren. And the children of Reuben and children of Gad and the half tribe of Ma-nas-seh, returned, and departed from the children of Israel out of Shi'-loh, which is in the land of Canaan, to go unto the country of Gil'-e-ad, to the land of their possession, whereof they were possessed, according to the word of the Lord by the hand of Moses. And when they came unto the borders of Jordan, that are in the land of Canaan, the children of Reuben and the children of Gad and the half tribe of Ma-nas'-seh, built there an altar by Jordan, a great altar to see to. And the children of Israel heard say, Behold, the children of Reuben and the children of Gad and the half tribe of Ma-nas'-seh have built an altar over against the land of Canaan, in the borders of Jordan, at the passage of the children of Israel. And when the children of Israel heard of it, the whole congregation of the children of Israel gathered themselves together at Shi'-loh, to go up to war against them.

And the children of Israel sent unto the children of Reuben, and to the children of Gad, and to the half tribe of Ma-nas'-seh, into the land of Gil'-e-ad, Pin'-e-has the son of E-le-a'-zar the priest, And with him ten princes, of each chief house a prince throughout all the tribes of Israel; and each one was an head of the house of their fathers among the thousands of Israel. And they came unto the children of Reuben, and the children of Gad, and the half tribe of Ma-nas'-seh, unto the land of Gil'-e-ad, and they spake with them, saying, Thus saith the whole congregation of the Lord, What trespass is this the ye have committed against the God of Israel, to turn away this say from following the Lord, in that ye have builded you an altar, that ye might rebel this day against the Lord? Is the iniquity of Pe'-or too little for us, from which we are not cleansed until this day, although there was a plague in the congregation of the Lord, But that ye must turn away this day from following the Lord? and it will be, seeing ye rebel to day against the Lord, that to morrow he will be wroth with the whole congregation of Israel.

Notwithstanding, if the land of your possession be unclean, then pass ye over unto the land of the possession of the Lord, wherein the Lord's tabernacle dwelleth, and take possession among us: but rebel not against the Lord, nor rebel against us, in building you an altar beside the altar of the Lord our God. Did not A'-chan the son of Ze'-rah commit a trespass in the accursed thing, and wrath fell on all the congregation of Israel? and that man perished not alone in his iniquity. Then the children of Reuben and the children of Gad and the half tribe of Ma-nas'-seh answered, and said unto the heads of the thousands of Israel, The Lord God of gods, the Lord God of gods, he knoweth, and Israel he shall know; if it be in rebellion, or if in transgression against the Lord, (save us not this day,) That we have built us an altar to turn from following the Lord, or if to offer thereon burnt offering or meat offering, or if to offer peace offerings thereon, let the Lord himself require it; And if we have not rather done it for fear of this thing, saying, In time to come your children might speak unto our children, saying, What have ye to do with the Lord God of Israel? For the Lord hath made Jordan a border between us and you, ye children of Reuben and children of Gad; ye have no part in the Lord: so shall your children make our children cease from fearing the Lord. Therefore we said, Let us now prepare to build us an altar, not for burnt offering, nor for sacrifice:

But that it may be a witness between us, and you, and our generations after us, that we might do the service of the Lord before him with our burnt offerings, and with our sacrifices, and with our peace offerings; that your children may not say to our children in time to come, Ye have no part in the Lord. Therefore said we, that it shall be, when they should so say to us or to our generations in time to come, that we may say again, Behold the pattern of the altar of the Lord, which our fathers made, not for burnt offerings, nor for sacrifices; but it is a witness between us and you. God forbid that we should reel against the Lord, and turn this day from following the Lord, to build an altar for burnt offerings, for meat offerings, or for sacrifices, beside the altar of the Lord our God that is before his tabernacle. And when Pin'-e-has the priest, and the princes of the congregation and heads of the thousands of Israel which were with him, heard the words that the children of Reuben and the children of Gad and the children of Ma-nas'-seh spake, it pleased them.

And Phin'-e-has the son of E-le-a'-zar the priest said unto the children of Reuben, and to the children of Gad, and to the children of Ma-nas'-seh, This day we perceive that the Lord is among us, because ye have not committed this trespass against the Lord: now ye have delivered the children of Israel out of the hand of the Lord. And Phin'-e-has the son of E-le-a'-zar the priest, and the princes, returned from the children of Reuben, and from the children of Goad, out of the land of Ca-naan, to the children of Israel, and brought them word again. And the thing pleased the children of Israel; and the children of Israel blessed God, and did not intend to go up against them in battle, to destroy the land wherein the children of Reuben and Gad dwelt. And the children of Reuben and the children of Gad called the altar Ed: for it shall be a witness between us that the Lord is God. (Joshua 22: 1-34)

Notice how Reubenites and the Gadites, and the half tribe of Manasseh made a stand that was in conflict with the rest Israel to the point that the rest of Israel wanted to make war against them. But being compelled by the spirit to build the altar God had given them a revelation that could not be disputed. In this is the awesome revelation that we will have times in our lives that we must make a stand for the righteousness of God and in that God will give us words to say to the those that come against us for our stand. But the key here is standing for the Lord and knowing when we hear the word of the Lord in our spirit. A pure word from the Lord is motivated by our anger nor our envy or any other emotional responds. It could be connected with the passion that the Lord has laid upon our hearts to fulfill the destiny forewhich God has called us for. But the true relationship in placing one in the position of hearing from God is by dedication and determination. In this the pure essence of God is pushed outward that man sees and knows that it must be God that has moved us to the point we are. In this movement God will use another to guide us to the position forewhich God wants us in.

This is very interesting to me because we get attached to the word of God and implement the word of God in our lives and in that transformation starts to mold us and move us. Interesting how God will give us an earthly person to attach ourselves to that releases the maturity of the word of God in our lives that grows us as it take seed. In that our churches and pastors become a great force for God because the people of God attaches themselves to them. In this we have to be moved by the spirit to fine the right place for us to grow in good ground. Sometimes the attachment is to the Lord and the Lord will lead us to a place of trouble not for testing but for edifying not only the man or woman of God but ourselves as well. In this we grow in faith because we are depending on God that our movement was directed by Him for a purpose even when the purpose is not clear unto us. Do you remember the situation between David and Saul? In that situation David would not dishonor Saul because he wanted to please God and placed his faith in God and stood on the word of God. But in the midst of this a very interesting thing happen that causes one to see how God will move us and guide us even in the midst of trouble to the place where He wants us regardless of the situation.

Remember that Saul is king at the time and is in pursuit of David forewhich we know that Saul is king over all Israel. But God has anointed David to be king now but Saul refuse to hear this within his spirit but David did not want to harm Saul because he knew that Saul was an anointed man of God. Now I want you to see this that their will be times in our journey that we will have choices to make that is in the realm of following man or being guided by the spirit. You might come across a situation that a family church forewhich your entire family grew up in and your mother or father expects you to go to that same church. But spiritually you are being lead somewhere else and this is tearing at your spirit. Maybe a family member is the pastor or a teacher, deacon, or what ever and being a family tradition that everyone goes to that church. But spiritually it is not for you and you are being lead by the spirit to go somewhere else where you are able to reach the spiritual level where you are lead to be. Out of tradition and out of oral principles that are based upon guilt we have to make the stand for the spiritual. You see the spiritual is the key to the determination and dedication that moves us to the place in our journey that carries us to the point where we need to be. The same thing happen to the tribes simply because legally the tribes was bound to the seat of the kingship that was occupied by Saul. But spiritually they were lead to the anointing of God to David, which most likely forced them to face the issue of legalism verses spiritually leadership. This is a very important issue simply because we not only face this within the church but as well on the job with our friends and our peers. So let us take a look at this.

The Bible says: Now these are they that came to David to Zik'-lag, while he yet kept himself close because of Saul the son of Kish: and they were among the mighty men, helpers of the war. They were armed with bows, and could use both the right hand and the left in hurling stones and shooting arrows out of a bow, even of Saul's brethren of Benjamin. The chief was A-hi-e'-zer, then Jo'-ash, the sons of She-ma'-ah the Gib'-e-ath-ite: and Je'-zi-el, and Pe'-let, the sons of Az'-ma-veth: and Ber'-a-chah, and Je'-hu the An'-toth-ite, And Is-ma'-iah the Gib'-e-on-ite, a mighty an among the thirty, and over the thirty: and Jer-e-mi'-ah, and Ja-ha'-zi-el, and Jo-ha'-nan, and Jos'-a-bad the Ged'-e-rath-ite, E-lu'-zai, and Jer'-i-moth, and Be-a-li'-ah, and Shem-a-ri'-ah, and Sheph-a-it'-ah the Har'-u-phite, El'-ka-nah, Je-is'-ah, and A-zar'-e-el, and Jo-e'-zer, and Ja-sho'-be-am, the Kor'-hites, And Jo-e'-lah, and Zeb-a-di'-ah, the sons of Jer'-o-ham of Ge'-dor.

And of the Gad'-ites there separated themselves unto David into the hold to the wilderness men of might, and men of war fit for the battle, that could handle shield and buckler, whose faces were like the faces of lions, and were as swift as the roes upon the mountains; E'-zer the first, O-ba-di'-ah the second, E-li'-ab the third, Mish-man'-nah the fourth, Jer-e-mi'ah the fifth, At'-tai the sixth, E-li'-el the seventh, Jo-ha'-nan the eighth, El'-za-bad the ninth Jer-e-l'-ah the tenth, Mach'-ba-nai the eleventh. These were of the sons of Gad, captains of the host: one of the least was over an hundred, and the greatest over a thousand. These are they that went over Jordan in the first month, when it had overflown all his banks; and they put to flight all them of the valleys, both toward the east, and toward the west. And there came of the children of Benjamin and Judah to the hold unto David. And David went out to meet them, and answered and said unto the, If ye be come peaceably unto me to help e, mine heart shall be knit unto you: but if ye be come to betray me to mine enemies, seeing there is no wrong in mine hands, the God of our fathers look thereon, and rebuke it.

Then the spirit came upon Am'-a-sai, who was chief of the captains, and he said, Thine are we, David, and on thy side thou son of Jesse: peace, peace be unto thee, and peace be to thine helpers; for thy God helpeth thee. Then David received the, and made them captains of the band. And there fell some of Ma-nas'-seh to David, when he came with the Phi-lis'-tines against Saul to battle: but they helped the not: for the lords of the Phi-lis'-tines upon advisement sent him away, saying, He will fall to his master Saul to the jeopardy of our heads. As he went to Zik'-lag, there fell to him of

Ma-nas'-seh, Ad'-nah, and Joz'-a-bad, and Je-di'-a-el and Mi'-cha-el, and Joz'-a-bad, and E-li'-hu, and Zil'-thai, captains of the thousands that were of Ma-nas'-seh. And they helped David against the band of the rovers: for they were all mighty men of valour, and were captains in the host. For at that time day by day there came to David to help him, until it was a great host, like the host of God. And these are the numbers of the bands that were ready armed to the war, and came to David to He'-bron to turn the kingdom of Saul to him according to the word of the Lord. (1Chronicles 12: 1-23)

Notice that in the same chapter 1Chronicles 12 verse number 38 it reads: "All these men of war, that could keep rank, came with a perfect heart to He'-bron, to make David king over all Israel: and all the rest also of Israel were of one heart to make David king." This is very important simply because they were moved with a perfect heart to follow the spirit instead of the law of man that brought a true since of peace about what they are doing. That is the key to the movement of the spirit that the peace of God is the surrounding force that gives evidence that this move is of God. The biggest revelation for you and I is that everyday is not going to be a great day simply because we will never be trial free but everyday is a good day. You see in the character "Determination and Dedication" we find the biggest key ever in our Christian walk and that is simply that yes Christ went through, which was our perfect example but the Gadites demonstrates that their needs to be a deeper look at that because of what we need to do in order to get through.

To be dedicated simply gives us the rising power to continue even when you see the enemy coming. To be completely sold out for God Almighty and walk in the fullness of that gives us a determined conviction that nothing will turn us from our mission. Did you miss it, let me reveal it to you, one deal with the heart the other deal with the mind, because the heart contains the master of the character so the spirit is already ready but you mind and heart has to come to agreement. You see my friends that God's revelation for our lives depends upon our Spirit being captivated by Him and submitting your Heart to be a housing place for Christ Jesus and giving your Mind over to the heart to control. This will cause you Members of the Body to be submissive to the authority of the Southside that was brought to the fullness in our spirits through the revelation of the inspired word by the Spirit of God unto the Apostle Luke.

We take this character as a building stone of life that represent our Savior, as well as we know that we can always improve within our character. These characters are the prize of being God's glory to mankind, Determination Dedication, Compassion in Action and Willingness. With that we can develop into the person we suppose to be, because Christ did exactly what He was supposed to do because the foundation was strong and that is what we must develop a strong foundation in the Lord. If we put it together it would look like something like this: I am a "Willing (Simeon)" person who will be "Dedicated and Determined (Gad)" to build such a relationship with Christ Jesus that I will be "Compassion in Action (Rueben)" to stand against the attacks of the enemy to be used to call forth another into that "Light." Remember that Gad brought forth the Determination and Dedication that it takes to emerge victorious in all situations and circumstances that the adversary uses to try and destroy us. In that we know that God uses those same things as elevation points in our life to grow our faith in Him. This causes a chain reaction turning one into a force to be reckon with in the spiritual realm. This in returns brings freedom not only to the person but all those they come in contact with.

We see the necessity to understand the Tribe of Gad in the essence of the revelation of the separation of God's chosen people. In this area we see that Gad held something that you and I need in order to overcome this physical plain with spiritual intervention that pushes transformation within us that prepares us to go to the next level. We have to be ready to give our whole self to the Lord and regardless of what comes our way we continue on. We seemed to be a people that want to hold on to our mistakes and condemn ourselves for those mistakes. But I want you to know that within the tribe of Gad they made mistakes and they made bad choices but in the growing and maturing steps they came to overcome their weakness. They came to point of reaching a level that their past would not hinder them in the growing spiritually and in that they fully embraced their destiny in Christ Jesus. Which is for you and I we have to put away our condemnation of ourselves letting others manipulate us by keep us hostage by our mistakes. We must be Dedicated and Determine to fulfill our destiny in Christ that we learn and grow from our mistakes.

I believe that the Apostle Luke feed off of that and came into the fullness of his destiny in Christ and it carried on even to the Apostle Paul forewhich know one could have put no better as the Apostle Paul pen a letter under the influence of the Spirit of God and was lead to write these words. The Bible says: Not as though I had already attained, either were already perfect: but I follow after, if that I may apprehend that for which also I am apprehended of Christ Jesus. Brethren I count not myself to have apprehended: but this one thing I do, forgetting those things which are behind, and reaching forth unto those things which are before. I press toward the mark for the prize of the high calling of God in Christ Jesus. (Philippians 3:12-14) Remember we are called to God's Glory and in this we are going to see how all this goes forward to the Apostle Luke.

The Apostle Luke

Interesting how God used a gentile and non-Jewish person to bring the Spirit of God upon to pen two letters in the New Testament that has such impact that moves us still today. In this we know that God was securing the knowledge that He wanted to bring salvation to the entire world. By using this Gentile God brought the Apostle Luke to the fullness of his destiny in Christ Jesus through difficulties as well as struggles within his own being to become the person forewhich God was able to use. We need to look at the life of Apostle Luke to see a few things that will give us great insight to the growing and understanding of the relationship between the Apostle Luke and the tribes. So let us begin.

The Apostle Luke was a fellow labor of the Apostle Paul and a physician as well as a historian. He was with the Apostle Paul on his missionary journeys that brought forth great deal of understanding of the revelation of God's word as well as a key essential to the development of his character. Now traditionally hold evidence that the Apostle Luke was from Antioch in Syria, which is possible, because Antioch played a significant role in Acts. Now Antioch of Syria is the capital of the Roan province of Syria which played a very important role in the first-century expansion of the church. It was situated on the east bank of the Orontes River, about 27 kilometers fro the Mediterranean Sea north of Jerusalem. The city was founded about 300 B. C. by Seleucus I Nicator, one of the three successors to Alexander the Great, and named for his father Antiochus.

Now the Apostle Luke accompanied Paul on parts of his second and third, and final missionary journeys. The Apostle Luke was most likely a humble man with no desire to blow his own horn or was looking for a pat on the back for his efforts in the progression of the Gospel through out the land. Just a little more than one-fourth of the New Testament comes fro his pen, but not once does he mention himself by name. He was very fluent in the Greek language and was probably more broad-minded and more refine than any other New Testament writer. He possessed a character that had been so tenderized through the connection with the Apostle Paul that brings us to the since that his ability to feel was much deeper than most. What I mean about his ability to feel is simply that he felt things much deeper than others as if he was absorbing the pain and the trials and situations of others and carried that pain with him. As saying if you hurt I hurt you are joyful I am joyful.

In the maturing of his character was build around faith and being faithful to another as they pursue their calling of Christ Jesus. By him being fluent in Greek and a historian his ability to pay attention to the details was increditable as well as his absorption of information simply because he was a doctor. In the building of his character the transformation of him seeing the things that was going on with the Apostle Paul and the rest of disciples caused a maturing that transformed him into a receiver and a deliver of the true essence of God. We know that at the time of Christ crucifixion the Apostle Luke was not present as well as we know that the

Apostle Luke was not perfect but the steady flow of maturity let us know that influence of the past did not bound him but he drew strength and learned from his mistakes.

Simply because we see that the Apostle Luke was surrounded by the men and women of God that influence him so much that he moved in a since of Compassion in Action (Reuben). We see in the writings of the Apostle Luke that being inspired by the Spirit of God he was lead to pen a letter to the "Most Excellent Theophilus." It seems to be a lot of controversy around Theophilus but for me it is that I see this man as one that was of high ranking most likely in the Roman government and it seems that the Apostle Luke wanted to give him the truth about the Man Christ Jesus from a particular view. He wanted to show the humanity of Christ, which reveals the true essence of Jesus Christ. This is the key to the revelation of the character of the Apostle Luke. Humanity is simply the fact or quality of being kind, tender, merciful etc. You see Christ moved by His humanity or the fact or quality of being kind, tender, merciful etc. simply because of the perfecting of the traits of Compassion in Action, being moved Willingness because of His Dedication and Determination to let the Father be seen to the world.

The Father mission for Christ was moved by the traits that govern the one word that explain the entire situation and circumstances of Christ and His mission that was given by the Father. Or better yet if we look at the meaning of the names of the character holders might give us a better insight to the key. Reuben means: "Behold a son" and Simeon means: "God hears" and Gad means: "good fortune." Now let us put it together: "Behold a son God hears good fortune. Now this is very powerful let us take a deeper look into this by breaking it down and putting it back again. That statement simply is saying: "To look at Jesus Christ, God give close attention for the purpose base on evidence favorable results." What a powerful revelation for you and I simply because this gives us the deep revelation of the true essence of Christ that is our calling that shows proof of His presence in our lives.

You see we must understand that the gospels gives a blueprint of the elevation of a spiritual level that comes forth in our presence where others can see that Christ is here. First the Apostle Matthew gives us the mindset forewhich we no that we have to renew our minds from the deep penetration of the adversary to think as Christ thought. This gives us power to move within the circumstances fully equipped to handle the adversary attack. The Apostle Matthew let us know that the very first thing need for us is the renewing of the mind the studying of God's word so that we can know how to think and the power of our thoughts. Our thoughts are the reflection of the dominant spirit in our lives and the connection to the feeding process of the spirit to grow it to become stronger than the flesh.

In that we see the word of God come alive in our own mind that if we stay in the word we are His disciples indeed we will know the truth and the truth will set us free. This also gives evidence in our mind through the word of God that there is no condemnation to those that are in Christ Jesus. This digs the pit forewhich our faith is based upon.

You see the deep seed of faith is planted so deeply within us through the word of God and we actually see with our own eyes that God is faithful and just in His word. The mindset has three interesting links that is transform within our character that releases the steps into the next level. Judah that is "Wisdom" and Issachar is "Humble" and Zebulun is "Compassion." These three traits works hand in hand in seeing the transformation of one renewing their mind through the word of God that links themselves to the standard of The Kingship of Christ. Understanding the kingship mentality is the standard needed to be raised when one is out of the will of God and in these three traits that Christ live perfectly gives us the power to rebel the adversary. Sometimes we are in need to be humble or have more compassion toward others that will break us free from the false illusion that the adversary has upon us. Then sometime we need to apply wisdom in a situation that is spiritual wisdom to overcome the adversary attack. In that we see that God raises the standard of kingship that gives us the tools to use within the midst of the trial to turn a situation from an attack to a blessing.

We see that God raises the Eastside of the Tabernacle that is the Lion banner that expels the trait of being humble as well as having compassion in the wisdom of God's word working in our lives. Once the mind is fixated upon the word of God and the kingship mentality then there is a connection that is developing toward the heart. Simply because we know that when we are dealing with the word of God we are feeding the spirit and the heart is being tenderize through the word of God turning a stone heart into flesh. This brings about the pricking of the heart and moves one to the understanding that Christ came as a servant of the Father. We see and feel in our heart that has been tenderized that we need to reach out to others and find our place in the Body of Christ. Now our mind and heart is coming together as one and transforming one into the pinnacle of Christ the Servant.

This brings us into the Apostle Mark that uncovered the servitude of Christ forewhich three traits becomes dominant in the transformation of one becoming a servant. A worker in the kingdom of God gives evidence that God's transformation is within my members. You see this is done out of a perfect heart that our doing is based upon the transformation of the purity of the essence of the word of God. We do this with out any reservation or anything attached to our service that takes away from Christ. The three traits are Ephraim (Knowledge) and Manasseh (Comfortable in knowing (who we are)) and Benjamin (Discipline in flesh). You see we have to continually study the word of God to gain knowledge that is wisdom when it is implemented in our lives. But knowledge is what we have to draw from in being comfortable in knowing exactly who we are in the Body of Christ. We truly understand and have knowledge that everyone cannot be the head or hand some have to be eyes ears working together to build one complete body. That body becomes an effective unit when it is controllable or has discipline in the flesh. When we working through the mindset of Christ we obtain the knowledge constantly searching and going deeper into the word of God finding out who we are. In that we become comfortable in whom we are so that we can step into the fullness of who God called us to be.

Then discipline ourselves over our flesh that we are able to be used as a vessel for the glorifying of God. You see our service edifies the Body of Christ as well as glorify God. In this we see how Christ demonstrated the fullness of these traits as the Apostle Mark uncovers this about Christ as he writes about the Service of Christ the worker the servitude of the Son of Man. This is the second stage of our growth forewhich gives us ammunition when the attacks comes the banner of the Ox is raised that brings forth the power of service of God that releases knowledge that can be drawn from and being comfortable to the knowledge of who we are as well as knowing when we are out of the will of God. Then being discipline enough to sacrifice our flesh daily that brings us closer to God. You see the Westside is the banner called upon by God when times of service become the weapon use to break us free from the bondage of the adversary. Now this fills our heart the service of God that propels us in our edifying of the Body of Christ to glorify God that we are moved to the next level spiritually that affect the physical.

In the process of the transformation of the heart from stone to flesh and the mind being constantly renewed by the word of God then something miraculous happens. Christ comes forth in a way that signifies the true essence of who He is. The Southside opens up and God explodes all around and the purity of which He is comes forth and others see this and they are affected. The Southside represents three traits forewhich Christ perfected Reuben (Compassion in Action) and Simeon (Willingness) and Gad (Dedication and Determination) which builds a great and wonderful thing that there is one word that describe the total package. You have to understand that the Apostle Luke wrote about Christ the Man the true essence of who He is by showing us His compassion in action and the willingness and the dedication and determination bring forth the one thing that God commands us to show and be which is "Love."

If I was to give one word for each side I would have to say that the Eastside the Apostle Matthew "Wisdom" and the Westside "Servant" and the Southside is "Love" that covers it completely. The Apostle Luke demonstrated the Love of God and the reason for the essence of Jesus Christ that is love. You see in the Apostle Luke development his character was overwhelmed by love for seeing the apostles' struggle in the presenting of the gospel. As the Apostle Paul being lead by the Spirit of God shown the Love of God through his action as he carried forth the gospel with power and vigor. In that we see that love is what God called us to be and show as well as become simply because this brings forth the true essence of the presence of God as well as showing the exact nature of who Jesus Christ.

This is what compelled the Apostle Luke being lead by the spirit to write a letter to a friend of the love of Jesus Christ by fulfilling the calling forewhich the Father had for his life. He wanted to be a witness to the truth of love and wanted his friend to know it was love that got Christ through. It was love that brought Christ forth in the first place. *God so loved the world that he gave his only begotten Son, that whosoever believeth in hi should not perish, but have everlasting life.* (John 3:16) If love is not in you then neither is Christ. Love is the key essential forewhich produces the true essence of whom we belong to. You see God loved us first and it is the love that moved the Apostle Luke to the position to be used by God to make such a magnitude upon you and I that it is still affecting us today. I say this all the time that if you want to learn to witness study the Gospel of Luke. You see it is the love that is the springboard forewhich our witness is power pact and not doing it out of a religious order. You see the witness is the most effective tool used to draw another out of the darkness but if our witness is just that a tool without the hammer of love behind it then it loses its power.

But if we are drawn to tell another about Christ out of love then the person see and feel the presence of God and the word of God goes forth to do exactly what it was meant to do. This is the working we see in the Apostle Luke writings to give an accurate description of the true essence of Christ Jesus out of Love for God and for his friend to bring forth a witness that is effective and productive. This is the mindset of the Apostle Luke and it is simply the most powerful force on the earthly plain, which is "Love" and this love is the true essence of whom Jesus Christ is and the exact reason forewhich the Father sent Him. The three elements that makeup the characteristics of love is "Compassion in Action" and "Willingness" as well as "Dedication and Determination." In this we see "Behold a son God hears good fortune" that releases a revelation for you and I that is "To look at Jesus Christ, God give close attention for the purpose base on evidence favorable results." Look at love and in love God pays close attention base upon the evidence of love whatever happens will be with favorable results for you. Simply because you sought the kingdom of God first and all other things will be added unto you that was glued together through a fusion of love that was expelled from you that attaches itself to the Heavenly Host. Remember that we are members of the Body of Christ that strives to produce an affective product that edifies and glorifies God in everything that we do.

How great of a testimony to bring forth the true essence of Christ Jesus in our everyday life and place this first in dealing with others. Knowing within ourselves that God love us even when we knew Him not. In that we see the magnitude of expressing and showing love in the purest of form without reservations or anything attached. Simply being moved by the transformation of the heart from stone to flesh which was initiated by the renewing of the mind that pushed the love of Christ outwardly to draw another out. Here is my testimony to you that you and I show more love toward all people that Christ's love explodes in everything that we do as well as everywhere we go till we place a positive mark on everyone. I was lead to write this book simply out of the love for the fellow members in the Body of Christ forewhich I wish the whole world became a part of to give revelation to the questions and stumbling blocks that causes one to stay in bondage. It is a book for those seeking a deeper relationship with Christ and to move unto the next level in their journey.

I want you to know that it is you that I wrote this material for and it is my sincere prayers that this becomes a stepping-stone for you to move upward in the spiritual journey that you are on. "Behold a son God hears good fortune" that simply means "To look at Jesus Christ (love), God gives close attention for the purpose (of love), base on evidence (love is shown) favorable results. Hold on to that for your ammunition when the adversary brings forth a mounted attack against you. I pray that God keeps the protection hedge around you and transform you to the true essence of Christ. I pray that love is the spring-board that gets you up in the morning seeking another to tell the true story of the birth, death, and burial as well as the resurrection of Jesus Christ that affectively penetrates the adversary bondage and bring another out of the land of darkness. A-men.

I know love is a very hard thing to maintain when the adversary is trying to keep us in hate and rebellion. But we have a blueprint now in the Bible to give us the keys and the principles to implement in our lives that attaches itself to the atmosphere of God. This attachment brings down the abundance of the heavens in our lives. Praise God for His word and for His perfect example in Jesus Christ, letting us know that we can and we will overcome. Have a bless day and remember God is love and love is God.

Made in the USA
Columbia, SC
28 May 2023